Construction Companion to Terms of Engagement and Fees

Richard J. Byrom

RIBA Publications

© Richard J. Byrom 2001

Published by RIBA Companies Ltd, which trades under the name of
'RIBA Publications', 1–3 Dufferin Street, London EC1Y 8NA

ISBN 1 85946 093 3

Product Code: 22593

Publisher: Mark Lane
Editor: Lionel Browne
Series Editor: David Chappell
Commissioning Editor: Matthew Thompson
Project Editor: Katy Banyard
Design: Bettina Hovgaard-Petersen

Typeset, printed and bound by Hobbs the Printers, Hampshire

Contents

Foreword

This is the second in a series of guides being produced by RIBA Publications under the general heading of *Construction Companion*. They are intended to be compact and accessible guides written in plain language, but each one authoritative about its own subject.

Understanding terms of engagement first requires the architect to understand the client. Clients come in all shapes and sizes and in many different forms of legal entity: from the householder at one end of the scale wanting more space in the house to a multi-billion-pound limited liability company requiring large new offices. It is a fact of life that the same architect is unlikely to act for both kinds of client at the same time. Each client is unique. If the architect knows the client's motives, it will be the key to many other aspects of each commission.

It is quite common for the architect to be unsure or mistaken about the identity of the client. This confusion inevitably surfaces when a dispute arises. Not knowing who is responsible for paying fees is a nightmare scenario if there are substantial fees outstanding. Architects have been known to get themselves into awkward situations, for example when a client says that it is arranged that some other person will pay the fee, or when the client is dependent upon a third party to provide funding.

Not only is it essential that the architect has a firm grasp of the procurement process and the standard form option available, it is also important to know what is available so far as terms of appointment are concerned and, especially, the implications of the various clauses and the way in which the proposed procurement system can influence the terms on which the architect and other professionals should carry out their services.

Collateral warranties, the limitation period, other disciplines, subcontractor design, variants on normal practice such as consultant switch, novation and taking over from another architect: guidance on all these topics and many more is to be found in the pages of this excellent little book. This should be the first (and sometimes last) point of reference for all architects about to enter into an engagement.

Richard Byrom has a wealth of knowledge and experience in this field. This is an extremely easy book to read, with checklists, bullet points and many enlightening thumbnail case studies.

David Chappell BA(Hons Arch) MA(Arch) MA(Law) PhD RIBA
Series Editor

Preface

Not so many years ago architects had it easy. There were fixed fees of 6% on new work and 10% on alteration work, no undercutting, no advertising, very few interviews, only a few competitions and those on strictly regulated terms and, in the main, only one procurement method, using JCT 63 or the JCT Minor Works Form. The architect was the undisputed lead consultant and kingpin of most building developments.

It was not so in the mid 19th century, and is not so again in the 21st century, for the pendulum has swung – the wheel has turned. The architect today faces a plethora of procurement methods in the drastic aftermath of the Thatcherite abandonment of fee scales and the longest and deepest recession, from 1989 to the mid 1990s, that any currently practising architect or builder had ever known. The architect is left to hack out a path through the jungle that is today's construction industry, taking care not to be mauled or bitten! Here are some of the changes and challenges:

- competition between architects for architectural work
- ludicrously low fee-bidding
- competition from other professions, notably building surveyors, for architectural work
- the introduction of a wide range of alternative procurement methods
- the blurring of the traditional divide between design and construction, seen not least in the large number of design and build projects
- competition for the role of lead consultant or adviser, not least from the sometimes parasitical project manager
- a lot of talk about partnering, some of it tongue in cheek
- the demise of the traditional general contractor
- the rise in various guises of the construction manager
- the rapid growth of labour-only and specialist subcontractors
- the proliferation of complicated standard forms of contract
- the requirement for increasingly complex buildings to be built ever faster and cheaper
- the growth of a voracious claims consultancy industry
- the advent of PFI and total life cycle costing
- an amazing belief in some circles that low cost, low risk, high speed and high quality are compatible
- the ever-developing law in an increasingly litigious environment
- architects beginning to provide contract management, management contracting and design and build services, or acting as developer as well.

Ours is a complex and high-risk industry. When things go wrong the consequences tend to be costly and stressful. The architect's risks can be very significantly reduced by understanding, defining and documenting the extent of his or her commission and terms of engagement. This book seeks to give some basic guidance in this area to the UK practitioner. It is written especially for those launching out into private practice and those newly appointed to senior positions in established practices of all types and sizes. Experienced practitioners should find it a useful short refresher course, and RIBA Part III students may find that it provides a useful insight into practice as it actually is. The book is written primarily with reference to architects, but it should also be of value to other consultants providing design and contract management services, including building surveyors, structural and civil engineers, M & E consultants and possibly even quantity surveyors.

RJB

Further reading

At the end of each chapter there are details of some books that may be useful for further reading. Those that I consider the more important, and which tend to be readily available, I have marked with an asterisk. The standard forms of building contract and standard forms of agreement between architect and client are referred to in the text, and are therefore not included in the further reading.

Acknowledgements

I acknowledge the gracious persistence of Matthew Thompson, the RIBA Publications commissioning editor; the wide knowledge and remarkable turn-round speed of Dr Chappell, the series editor; and above all my secretary, Mrs Jackie Moloney, who has typed the numerous drafts with patience and competence. Thanks too to my colleagues at Byrom Clark Roberts, the practice of which I am privileged to be a part.

1   Entering into a contract

The three elements that make up a contract are an *offer*, an *acceptance* and a *consideration*. The architect offers to design a building and administer the building contract for a consideration, normally money. The client accepts the offer and undertakes to pay the consideration.

A contract does not need to be in writing; or it may be in writing but no more than a mere sentence:

> *Dear Joe, I write to confirm our agreement that I will be the architect for your new building at 6%. Yours, Archie.*

In either case architects lay themselves wide open to:

- being unable to recoup proper remuneration for their efforts
- finding that they have undertaken far greater liabilities than they intended to
- falling out with their clients
- spending an inordinate amount of time, and probably money, on stressful disputes.

It must be obvious to even the most naïve young architect that the confirmation of an appointment in the above terms may lead to problems in answering any of the following questions:

- Who are the contracting parties?
- What building is to be designed?
- What is meant by '*be the architect*'?
- Is the design of structural elements and services included?
- What form of building contract is anticipated – traditional procurement or WCD98?
- 6% of what?
- Are expenses in addition to the 6%?
- Does the 6% include VAT?
- Has the architect undertaken to obtain planning permission?
- Is the architect to pay the planning and building regulation fees?
- At what stages are fees to be paid?
- Is the architect to carry unlimited liability?
- Can the architect get out of his or her obligations if the client is totally unreasonable?

It is all so obvious that this book might well be shelved now, and the time given to fee-earning work. If only it was so! Any architect who knows a lawyer involved in professional indemnity work or a fellow architect who undertakes expert witness work will know the sad truth that some otherwise brilliant architects are clueless when it comes to their own contractual arrangements. Getting these arrangements in order at the right time will not of course protect an architect against claims for wrong technical design or the failure to issue the production information on time; nor will it adequately protect the architect in the event of the liquidation of the client. But it will assist the architect in getting paid and in avoiding many time-consuming and stressful claims as, once a building contract goes wrong, and sadly many do, the building owner will seek to recover whatever he can from whoever he can, and there are few more certain ways to invite a claim than to have to sue for fees.

In summary it is the following that have to be clearly set out:

- the parties
- the services to be provided
- the consideration for those services
- the terms and conditions relating to the contract.

Let a keen student lawyer loose on your fee agreement and you will end up with a document more like a bill of quantities, covering every eventuality, and the client will go somewhere else! Every job is different, and the skill is to assess what is required for each commission to reasonably secure and protect the architect's position. The exercise is akin to risk assessing. What is appropriate for a multi-million-pound fast-track project will be inappropriate for a bathroom extension for a disabled person, and vice versa. This is recognised in that there are various RIBA standard forms of agreement for different circumstances.

It is broadly the position that the architect's responsibilities in contract last for six years, usually from practical completion, if the contract is under hand or 12 years if executed as a deed. In addition to responsibilities in contract, the architect may have parallel responsibilities to the client in tort, particularly the tort of negligence, and also in certain circumstances to third parties who might rely upon the architect's statements or work. Damages in tort, in construction cases, exclude the *purely financial losses* of the defect itself but not necessarily the losses that it causes to other persons or property. There may also be liability, both to client and/or third parties, where there has been reliance upon *negligent misstatements,* which can include incorrect drawings, and in respect of personal injuries. In tort the time limit is initially six years from the negligent act but thereafter three years from when the claimant should reasonably have been aware of the problem, usually with a long stop of 15 years from the breach of duty. In some cases, for example where indemnities or warranties have been given, it can be longer.

Further reading

V. Powell-Smith and D. Chappell (eds) *Building Contract Dictionary* 3rd edn (Blackwell Science, 2001).

S. Furst (ed.) *Keating on Building Contracts* 7th edn (Sweet & Maxwell, 2001).

*A. Speaight and G. Stone (eds) *Architect's Legal Handbook* 7th edn (Architectural Press, 2000).

2 The architect: the service provider

2.1 The solo practitioner

It is not unusual for a well-known practice, often bearing the name of its original principal, to have been set up by a single architect launching out, taking a small office and putting up his or her plate. Some who so launch remain solo practitioners, often by choice.

In mid career some architects in large and highly pressured practices find themselves the casualties of one or other recession, with its inevitable redundancies, and make the decision to set up on their own away from the big city in an area where sparsity of work may be compensated for by quality of life, often working from an office attached to or within the home. There are many such, for example, in the Lake District. Similarly there are those mid-career architects who choose to leave their large, highly pressured city centre practices because they have experienced the stress of major projects and have noted that this can so easily lead to marital breakdown, psychiatric problems or worse. They experience the lure of a small practice with low overheads in a superb environment.

Later on in life there are those who take early retirement from their busy practices in order to concentrate on specialities such as dispute resolution, acting as expert witness, adjudicator or arbitrator, often from an office at home.

There are many advantages in being a solo practitioner:

- One does not have to consider partners or co-directors.
- One can work as much or as little as one chooses, and one's rewards follow accordingly.
- One can take on or turn away work as one pleases.
- There is no possibility of partnership fallouts, or of the problems that occur when a partner under-performs.

There are also considerable disadvantages for the solo practitioner:

- There is no one to share ideas with, to crit designs or to bounce ideas off. For these reasons it is a short-sighted solo practitioner who does not play an active part in local RIBA branch or other professional bodies.
- It is difficult to keep up with changes in practice. These come on every front, faster and faster every year. A solo practitioner, and indeed any architect, needs to allocate time for reading and filing articles from professional journals, and needs to have ready access to a substantial professional library, such as the

computerised *Barbour Construction Expert* or the RIBA's *Technical Indices*, which are far more comprehensive than most traditional architects' libraries, including for example all the British Standards applicable to construction.

- Standard 9 of the *ARB Code of Professional Conduct and Practice* states:
  The fact that an Architect has not maintained his professional competence may count against him in the event of that competence having to be investigated.
  The RIBA *Standard of Professional Performance* appended to the RIBA *Code of Professional Conduct* states at 6 that the architect is required:
  When in practice as a sole practitioner or sole principal to make reasonable attempts to establish professional contact with other Members which could provide opportunities for the mutual exchange of experience and knowledge.

- There are problems during holidays and illness. Building contracts do not stop when the architect is on holiday or ill. Queries still have to be answered. The RIBA *Standard of Professional Performance* includes the following requirement at 4:
  To make arrangements with an appropriately qualified person for the running of their offices and administration of contracts during a period of absence and inform clients of those arrangements.
  The appropriate qualifications will depend upon the work being undertaken. The obvious solution is a reciprocal arrangement between two solo architects who trust each other, but an arrangement with a chartered building surveyor or a very experienced architectural technician may be appropriate in some cases. Details of the arrangements should be briefly formalised, giving the person providing cover written authority to act as agent for the architect in the latter's absence, be it on holiday or in the event of a sudden accident or illness, or even death.

2.2 The partnership

A partnership has the reverse benefits and drawbacks from those of the solo practice described above.

There is the additional problem that within a partnership (and this may involve those whose names are on the notepaper but remain only salaried partners) each partner is jointly and severally liable for all the debts of the practice, and actions taken by one partner will bind all the partners. Furthermore, if partnerships do not work, their dissolution may be very bitter and costly.

Essential starting points in a partnership are to know those with whom one is to enter into partnership, and to have a partnership agreement drawn up by a solicitor, who will advise on the many potential problem areas that need to be covered.

There are particular concerns for an older partner in a small partnership, which need to be thought through when a partnership agreement is entered into. They include the following:

- The modern tendency is no longer to see a partnership as an engagement for the remainder of a career. This is particularly noticeable in the legal profession, where able younger partners tend to transfer to other practices, often taking their team and clients with them. These were perhaps the people whom the older partners were looking to to pay off their partners' loan accounts and goodwill. Now the younger partner has staked a claim to available monies, and the soon-to-retire partners may be in great difficulties.
- The problem of getting money out of a practice is compounded when two partners, perhaps friends from university days who started the practice, come to retirement at around the same time. There may be nobody else in the practice, or outside it, able and/or willing to take on the practice.
- If this is the case, the retiring partners have the problem (as does a solo practitioner in the same position) of having to purchase run-off professional indemnity cover for 15 years: that is, to the limit of their liability in tort (or longer if unwise warranties have been entered into). This is vital, as a retired partner may find him or herself being sued many years after ceasing practice.

2.3 The limited liability company

Most medium-sized and larger practices now practice as limited liability companies. This means that the chances of being made bankrupt for an error or oversight that is not of one's own doing are significantly reduced, and one's personal assets are reasonably safeguarded.

Limited liability status will not necessarily protect architects from their own errors, as they can in some circumstances be sued in tort, as individual directors of the practice.[1] Thus an architect who has substantial assets should take legal and accountancy advice.

Disadvantages of trading as a limited liability company might be:

- some financial disadvantage in certain circumstances
- because annual accounts have to be filed at Companies House, and copies are available to the public, the fact that some details of one's financial situation will be in the public domain.

Advantages include:

- increased protection of personal assets
- ease of transfer of shares, and thus ease of bringing in new shareholders.

2.4 The limited liability partnership

Up until 2001, those who wished to limit their liability normally did so by trading as limited liability companies. From April 2001 there is legislation to permit *limited liability partnerships*. Architects who are not currently trading as limited liability companies, but who are considering doing so, should discuss this alternative with their solicitor and accountant.

2.5 The cooperative

There are various types of cooperative, which are beyond the scope of this work. Those who hold themselves out as *non-profit-making* may be seeking an unfair advantage, as many limited liability practices or partnerships show no profit after paying a fair salary to their directors.

2.6 The group practice

There are many forms of group practice, the most common of which are:

- associations of independent firms that share experience and knowledge, and sometimes undertake joint marketing
- groups of two or more firms that share accommodation, facilities, equipment and perhaps secretarial staff
- firms that come together to undertake a single commission or to provide wide geographical coverage to a particular client.

Further reading

*D. Chappell and A. Willis *The Architect in Practice* 8th edn, Chapters 3 and 4 (Blackwell Science, 2000).

*S. Cox and A. Hamilton *Architect's Handbook of Practice Management* 6th edn (RIBA Publications, 1998).

F.A. Paterson and P. Britton *Limited Liability Partnerships: A Guide for Professionals* (Kings's College London, 2001).

Notes

1 See *Merrett v Babb*, Times 27.07.01. See also *Williams & Anor v Natural Life Health Foods Ltd* [1998] 2 All ER 577.

3 The client: the purchaser of the architect's services

Just as the architect can be an individual, partnership or limited liability company, so can the client: indeed there are several more options, as clients may include any of the following.

3.1 The individual client

This is normally the most straightforward, but an architect should beware of the individual who writes his or her letters on notepaper of a limited liability company.

Example

An architect took instructions to design a substantial extension to a private house. The client asked that all correspondence be sent to his office, as this would ensure a quicker reply, because he had a secretary to do his typing. All the replies came on the notepaper of his limited liability company. When tenders were received, the client explained that he could not proceed as he was experiencing financial difficulties. The architect sued for his considerable outstanding fees, only to receive the reply that his contract was with the limited liability company (which, as part of its MD's remuneration package, provided the MD's house), and unfortunately the company had called in the receiver.

3.2 The partnership

Partners are jointly and severally liable.

When undertaking work for a law or accountancy partnership it is prudent to get the client to sign the agreement *for self and partners*. For other partnerships, where the status may be less obvious, it is prudent to get signatures from each partner. This is also the case with a married couple or domestic partnership.

Example

The lady partner of a successful businessman commissioned designs for alterations and extensions to their home. By the time the architect had sued for his fees, she had eloped to South America with someone else, and her partner said he knew nothing about the designs and was not interested in them.

3.3 The trading name

Many individuals, partnerships and limited companies use trading names that are not legal entities. Most architects would advise their client against entering into a contract with AA1 Roofing Specialists whose notepaper looked impressive but contained a PO box address and a mobile telephone number. Yet some architects fall for this one, perhaps on a much grander scale.

3.4 The limited liability company

Here the important point is for the architect to make sure that this contract is with the right limited liability company. It is no good entering into a contract with *Building Today Limited* if the correct client name is *Building Today (1999) Limited,* especially if there are several other companies with a similar name but a different year! Agreements with a limited liability company should be signed by a director and/or the company secretary, whose positions should be noted against their signatures.

Many companies have subsidiaries, and there is sometimes confusion as to which company or subsidiary is entering into the contract. It *does* matter!

3.5 The limited liability partnership

If the client partnership is a limited liability partnership it is important to know this and to proceed accordingly: see below.

3.6 The public liability company

In the main these are the bigger companies, but often the architect's contract will be with a subsidiary, and a parent company guarantee may be needed.

3.7 Charities

Charities must be registered with the Charities Commission. Most charities have trustees, sometimes drawn from the great and the good and sometimes local bigwigs, but the day-to-day administration is undertaken by executives and officials. It is important for the architect to ensure that the person he or she is dealing with has the appropriate authority to act on behalf of the charity. Because the trustees hold the money, the architect's contract will normally be with the trustees. Some private schools are charities, although the architect's contract may be with the governors.

Many religious organisations are charities, and in most cases the architect's contract will need to be with the body that owns or is going to own the building. This needs care. If there are trustees, the architect's contract may be with all the trustees individually. Work on Church of England buildings will normally be for the vicar and PCC.

3.8 Clubs

Most clubs – for example sports clubs, working men's clubs, political clubs or gentlemen's clubs – will have trustees, and the contract will normally be with the trustees. In the cases of charities or clubs it is highly desirable that there is one named person properly authorised to communicate with the architect on behalf of the organisation.

3.9 Checking out the client

Having established who the client is to be, the next thing is to ensure that the client is going to be able to pay.

For small clients of dubious standing it may be appropriate to ask for *money up front*. Solicitors do this as a matter of course, but most architects find it somewhat distasteful. They should contemplate the alternative of not getting paid. However, if money is to be obtained in advance, it is necessary to have a properly constituted clients' account and to ensure that the money stays in that account until invoiced. Members' rules for clients' accounts are set out at the back of the RIBA *Code of Professional Conduct.*

The Housing Grants, Construction and Regeneration Act 1996 (HGC&RA) gives provisions for the suspension of work in the event of non-payment of invoices. This is an important provision, but it is obviously best if it can be avoided, and one way is to send small but regular invoices, rather then letting large ones build up. The adjudicator and payment provisions of HGC&RA are specifically excluded from contracts with residential occupiers, but SFA/99 or SW/99 need not necessarily be amended provided both parties agree the provisions can remain and apply. The model letter of appointment in SW/99 includes the following:

> *We have agreed that in the unlikely event of a dispute or difference arising under this Agreement, without prejudice to any right of adjudication, it shall be referred to arbitration…*

So far as limited liability companies are concerned, it is relatively easy to obtain copies of the last filed accounts from Companies House, but these may of course be out of date. In addition one can ask one's bank to take up a banker's reference, which, if read between the lines, may ring warning bells; or one can buy advice from a firm that provides credit ratings.

Where the client company or limited liability partnership looks dubious, options are to ask for a parent company guarantee (when there is a parent company), or to ask for the contract to be with the directors. This may lose the client, but if it does it may have saved the architect from a much greater loss later on!

3.10 The experienced client

Many clients are building all the time. These include local authorities, banks, building societies, breweries, hotel chains, supermarket companies, housing associations, and well-established development companies. In the main they will have in-house construction professionals looking after their building programmes, with laid-down procedures. They are likely to be demanding, but for the architect who performs there is likely to be repeat business.

3.11 The inexperienced client

Even with what one would expect to be an experienced client, difficulties can occur when the in-house manager given the task of running the building project does not have construction experience, or where an inexperienced professional wants to earn the favour of his financially motivated superiors by showing that he has beaten professional fee levels down. Top-flight service and rock-bottom fees are incompatible; but there are always inexperienced whizz-kids around who have yet to learn this simple lesson.

There are many clients who will have had little or no experience of building. For many households, small businesses and clubs, a building project is a new experience. For some it will not be a happy experience, and in those cases the architect will also suffer.

The following are some of the many measures that may help towards a successful project when working with an inexperienced client, particularly when that client is a committee:

- The architect needs to explain to the client how building procedures operate. Committees are amongst the most difficult of all clients, but an evening spent explaining procedures to the whole of the committee will often be time well spent, not least in building the committee's confidence in its architect.

- The architect will do well to persuade a client committee to delegate its powers to a very small subcommittee. At least by doing this the architect is in with some chance, but any architect who finds him or herself dealing with a large committee, particularly one whose members are not used to dealing with professional people, needs to increase the fee percentage to compensate for the time and effort, often outside normal working hours, needed to work closely with, and retain the confidence of, the client committee.
- A prudent architect records everything – minutes of all meeting and attendance notes of all telephone calls – and circulates the records to all involved. Of course this should be done for each and every job, whoever the client, but never is it more important than when dealing with a committee. The committee might have completely changed before the project is finished!

A particular difficulty with clubs and charities is the member who wants to help and is sure he can twist arms to get gifts of tiles, slates, sanitary fittings or light fittings, and the keen members who want to do some of the work themselves! It is not unusual for such clients to initiate 'clever' schemes to save money and find that they are paying more.

Example

A cultural organisation decided to omit the light fittings in a new assembly room, and to introduce downlighters from a sympathetic supplier who would provide the fittings 'at cost'. When the fittings arrived, the electrician could not insert them into the ceiling void. Alternatives had to be obtained. There was a delay in getting the alternatives. Work to the floor finishes was held up by the installation of the lights. The claim was many times the saving.

Another particularly difficult client is the inexperienced developer, the real 'know-all' who believes he can run the job himself using smaller contractors and labour-only tradesmen, and who changes the plans as the job proceeds. When he runs out of money this client will probably blame the architect. Any architect who meets such a client should be extremely cautious. The following points may assist:

- The contractual arrangements should be agreed with the client in writing on day 1: this is the central message of this book. In particular the architect needs to set out exactly what will be done and what will not be done. It may also help to set out what others will do.
- Small invoices should be sent regularly, and there should be insistence on them being paid within the stated timescale. If necessary, cash flow problems should be spelt out and cheques collected in person.

- The HGC&RA provisions, notably adjudication, should be used if payments are delayed.
- Extreme caution needs to be exercised about taking on the role of planning supervisor – it could develop into a nightmare.
- It should not be forgotten that when the client gets into a mess he will say that he is an inexperienced layperson, who engaged an architect to assist him; he relied on his architect, but his architect did not advise him and thus must be responsible for the mess. To some extent he may be right.

3.12 Architects as their own clients

Sometimes it is galling for an architect to see a developer client make a huge financial success of a development, not least because of the skill and vision of the architect, who may be paid a pittance. One answer, adopted by some architects, is to become a property developer, perhaps initially in the design and construction of the architect's own office. There are risks, of course, and the effort and skills required to see through a successful development are considerable. Architects should be wary of believing that the grass is always greener on the other side.

The swashbuckling, cavalier approach that is sometimes in evidence in successful developers does not lie comfortably with the much more meticulous approach of the professional. But for those who can do it, this is one way to put the architect in the driving seat and ensure that design is not compromised.

In this respect the following words about architects are challenging:

> They are the Cinderellas of the construction industry, the one profession currently protected by statutory registration. Historically, this legislation has had a seriously inhibiting effect on what registered architects were able to do, in stark contrast to other countries where architects have dominated the field of construction professionals. This is changing in the UK, but architects are nevertheless way behind the field when it comes to new and innovative career patterns.[1]

Perhaps this will not be so in the future?

3.13 Clients best avoided

Clients best avoided include the following:

- 'clever, know-all' clients
- clients who want everything on the cheap and will not pay proper fees

- perfectionists, unless they are prepared to pay for perfection
- clients who cannot pay their bills
- clients who think it smart not to pay their bills
- unscrupulous clients
- clients who wish to do something dishonest or illegal. The most common areas are likely to be:
  - payment in cash to avoid VAT
  - work on a private residence to be invoiced through a company building project
  - the client who wants to do work without statutory approvals
- clients who require the architect to do an immense amount of work 'at risk' – for example no fee until and unless the building contract is signed.

The greatest caution is necessary in discussing budgets and timescales. Some clients will have impossible timescales and absurd budgets. The architect meeting such a client is faced with a dilemma. If the architect says what he or she knows to be the truth the client may look elsewhere, and will undoubtedly find some less scrupulous practitioner who will appear to concur with the client's whims, at least until the client is safely signed up. Given an educated and reasonable client there are unlikely to be any problems, but not all clients are educated and reasonable. Given the other sort of client, the architect may be better off without him or her.

Good reasons for not accepting a commission are as follows:

- The client is unsatisfactory (see above).
- The architect has not got the necessary experience or resources (see section 6.1 in Chapter 6).
- There will be conflict with the architect's design integrity or philosophy:
  - The client may want a mock Tudor, Gothic or Greek design from a practice that is making its name with hi-tech modern design.
  - The client may wish to undertake work to a listed building that the architect considers out of sympathy with that building and contrary to his or her conservation philosophy.
  - The architect's personal convictions may make him or her an inappropriate person to undertake the work. It is not difficult to think of some examples that could form the basis of scripts for comedy films, although in practice they tend not to occur.

Further reading

*S. Cox and A. Hamilton *Architect's Handbook of Practice Management* 6th edn, Chapters E and F (RIBA Publications, 1998).

*J.W.E. Masterman *An Introduction to Building Procurement Systems*, Chapter 7 (E & FN Spon, 1992).

Notes

1 J. Uff *Are We all in the Wrong Job? Reflections on Construction Dispute Resolution*, p. 4 (Society of Construction Law, 2001).

4   The project

Sometimes clients are very sure what they want, but the architect can see at a very early stage that it is not what they need.

Sometimes clients know that they want something, but are not sure what.

It is a prudent client who brings the architect in right at the beginning to help establish the brief, and who is prepared to pay for Work Stages A and B on a time basis.

Example

A church advised its architect that it needed a 300-seater building. With encouragement from the experienced church architect, the parish was persuaded to do an audit plotting attendance figures over the previous decade, and to assess future likely gains against future likely losses. When this was done it became abundantly clear that a building of half the size was likely to be more than adequate.

The more sophisticated and experienced clients will know what they need. They will probably have a detailed brief and established cost limits to go with it. The unknowns may be limited to the ground conditions and the restraints and requirements of the local planning authority.

Sometimes the project will hinge upon whether planning permission can be obtained.

Examples

The proprietors of a hotel, a listed building situated in green belt, wanted a substantial extension. It was clear that the size of the project would be limited to what the planners would allow.

The owner of another hotel, in an urban location, wished to demolish it and redevelop the fairly large site with flats. The hotel was not listed, but it had a fine façade that the planners wished to be retained. An alternative approach, but considerably less attractive from a financial point of view, was to convert the hotel into flats and build some low-rise properties in the grounds.

To assess a project in order to decide whether to take on the commission or not, on what terms and conditions and for what fees, one ideally needs to know:

* the type of building
* the size of the building

- the constructional system proposed
- the budget costs
- the timescale
- the procurement method
- the other consultants to be engaged
- the services required of the architect.

With the above information the architect can:

- assess whether the practice has adequate professional, financial and technical competence and resources
- assess the fees required
- enter into an appropriate contract for architectural services with written terms of engagement, probably using a standard form of agreement.

Without all the above information it may still be possible to enter into a standard form of agreement, as discussed in Chapter 9, but in any event it is vital to get terms agreed in writing for whatever limited services are known at the time work commences (see Chapter 10).

Further reading

D. Hyams *Construction Companion to Briefing* (RIBA Publications, 2001).

5 The initial approach

The initial approach from a prospective client may come in many ways, including:

- direct approach by the client
- competitive interview
- fee tender (without design)
- design submission with fee proposal
- design ideas competition.

Sometimes the approach will be for architectural services only, and sometimes for a package of consultancy services.

It is very difficult to respond adequately to any enquiry without some knowledge of:

- the type and size of project
- the timescale
- the procurement method.

The main factors in arriving at the level of fees are size of project, type of building, and procurement method.

On receipt of an initial enquiry, the following are some of the matters to be taken into consideration:

- Decide who is going to lead the practice response.
- Find out about the client:
  - Look at their website.
  - Make discreet enquiries as to how they treat people with whom they conduct business, if they can be trusted and if they pay on time.
- Speed of response. This is important.
- Note tender deadlines. These must be met or all the effort will be wasted.
- Who is the competition likely to be? If known, look at their websites and find out their strengths and weaknesses.
- What are likely to be the client's priorities:
  - good design?
  - proven track record?
  - low fees?
  - green issues?
  - political issues?
- If the potential client has recently undertaken building work, why do they want to change their design team?

- In the interview, who is going to present the practice?
- Will the client want to see the team leader?
- For a personal presentation, what is the appropriate dress?
- How many people will be at the presentation?
- How long is the presentation to last?
- How will the architect present him or herself and the practice to best advantage?
- What equipment will be available?
- If no equipment is available, will there be time to set it up: for example Powerpoint, overhead projection or display boards?
- Will the architect take a portfolio or folder of drawings and/or photographs and commendations from previous clients?

Disasters can occur at presentations to potential clients. For example:

- The architect relies on Powerpoint, but it fails. A necessary precaution is to have OHP transparencies as back-up.
- The architect relies on a slide projector or OHP, and the bulb fails. Ensure that a spare bulb is available.
- The architect relies on slides when there is no adequate black-out, and the sun is shining.
- The architect relies on any electrical equipment, only to find that there is no socket outlet nearby. It is essential to have a long lead available.
- The architect relies on presentation by way of drawings, but there is nowhere to display the drawings, or they are too small for the large committee to see.
- The architect arrives late. This is not a good start, and because one is rushed and stressed things may go from bad to worse. This risk is easily avoided by making allowances for contingencies, such as roadworks, tailbacks, punctures, late trains, getting lost, parking difficulties, or even being unable to find the venue. The best advice is to go early, find the venue, and then go for a walk or a coffee and read through one's notes. One can then arrive on time, relaxed and in control.
- Non-arrival: people do sometimes go to interviews at the wrong time, or on the wrong day, or at the wrong venue!

When tendering, especially if entirely on the basis of fees, it is important to tailor the quote to precisely the services requested, even if these are incomplete. To do more may mean a competitive disadvantage.

In the case of design submissions with fee proposals, the usual arrangement is for a small number of firms to be invited to bid against the same enquiry, and clients should expect to pay a fee to all tenderers who submit detailed design ideas. Architects taking part in such an arrangement will be wise to secure a formal agreement with the client, and, because getting damages for breach of copyright is never easy, it may be prudent to include a clause that if the design is used and the architect is not appointed to provide further services, a premium payment incorporating a specified licence fee for the copy and use of the design will be payable.

Increasingly, and quite properly, it is being appreciated by clients that value for money requires consideration of technical competence and design skills as well as fee levels. The initial criteria may exclude fees altogether; once the architect is chosen fees will be negotiated, another architect being approached only if those negotiations fail. Some selection processes have weightings for technical or design competence and fees.[1]

Undertaking speculative work *at risk* needs to be treated with great caution. Speculative work must be kept under strict control, not least the proportion of speculative work to fee-earning work being undertaken in the office at any one time. Work on a speculative basis should never be undertaken unless the architect is confident that if unsuccessful it will not have any serious effect on the practice. Vital matters to set out in the initial fee agreement are:

- exactly what work will be done at risk
- exactly what will trigger the change from working 'at risk' to working on a fee-earning basis
- what fees will be paid for the work done 'at risk' following the activation of that trigger
- what further services the architect will then be engaged to perform, for what fees, and on what terms and conditions
- what premium payment will be made to the architect if not so engaged
- whether any such premium will incorporate a licence fee for the copy and use of the design and, if so, whether the premium will be payable whether or not the design is adopted as a basis for the project.

Typical speculative work situations include:

- Competitions. Ideally these should be under the auspices of the RIBA Competitions Office. They should be *two-stage* with at least some fees paid to all the second-stage participants. The big risk with competitions is that the commission may not be placed with the winner: read the small print! Statistically the chances of winning a competition are small.
- Work for a developer who is bidding for a site and is looking for work to be done on a no win, no fee basis.
- Work for a contractor who is bidding for a design and build project and is similarly looking for the work to be done on a no win, no fee basis.

- Work for a housing association that is bidding for funds and wants the design work done for nothing on the basis that it will commission the architect if its bid is successful.
- Work for a charity submitting for a grant, without which the project will not go ahead. Sometimes the charity is looking for this initial work on a free basis – and there can be a lot of work involved.

Most prudent practices will undertake speculative work sparingly. The exceptions are those practices that have established working relationships with existing clients and who know they are likely to be commissioned for say one in three speculative projects at fee levels that adequately cover the abortive speculative work.

A real danger of speculative work is that, after a successful bid on the basis of the architect's drawings, the client then changes the consultancy team.

Example
A client engaged a high-profile architect whose standing would undoubtedly assist in the obtaining of planning permission. There was no formal fee agreement but an understanding that if successful the architect would be commissioned for the project. Once that permission was achieved the architect was paid a nominal sum and dumped.

Thus the need to have a proper agreement.

One should avoid going after what have been aptly called *rainbow projects:*

> A multi-million pound project to drill for inkwells in China for a new client who is developing all over the world is too exciting to turn down… avoid chasing rainbows!… If it goes ahead, will the fees you earn (assuming you get paid) justify the risk you have taken? There is no point doing nine-tenths of the work on spec to earn the other one-tenth if the project proceeds...[2]

In any event, speculative work is rarely in the interests of the client, and this needs to be proclaimed forcefully by the profession. It is almost inevitable that corners will be cut; the brief may not be properly developed, and initial planning may not receive the consideration that it should have. Rather, the emphasis is likely to be on a slick and colourful presentation, prepared to titillate the undiscriminating client. Can it realistically be otherwise if the architect is not being paid?

In any initial discussions, fee levels are likely to be aired, and great caution is needed. It is extremely dangerous to guess at fee levels if the information needed to compute the fee properly is not to hand. Indeed it can be fatal. If the guess is too high – no appointment. If it is too low – disaster for the architect! Other areas in which caution is necessary at the initial stage include:

- *The making of unwarranted claims in sales literature.* A consultancy had a brochure that said, in effect, 'We will manage your project to complete it on time and on budget.' The development was not on time, and far from on budget. The practice was subsequently sued on the basis that the inexperienced lay client had relied on the assurances given in the practice brochure, and that it was on the basis of those assurances that the client had actually chosen the particular practice!
- *The giving of unqualified assurances in interviews.* It is likely that someone will be preparing notes of what is said, or the interview may be recorded. It should be kept in mind that the first figures mentioned in respect of fees, or building costs, or the project timetable are likely to be the ones that will be remembered!

Where insufficient information is to hand to enter into, for example SFA/99, it is important to enter into a pre-SFA agreement setting out exactly what preliminary work is to be done and on what terms and conditions, as discussed later in Chapter 10.

Further reading

Construction Industry Board, Working Group 4 *Selecting Consultants for the Team: Balancing Quality and Price* 2nd edn (Thomas Telford, 2000).
RIBA *Engaging an Architect: Guidance for Clients to Quality Based Selection* (RIBA, 1999).
*S. Cox and A. Hamilton *Architect's Handbook of Practice Management* 6th edn, Chapter B2–7 on Marketing (RIBA Publications, 1998).
*S. Lupton (ed.) *Architect's Job Book* 7th edn, pp 15–30 (RIBA Publications, 2000).
C. McGhie and R. Girling *Architectural Competitions: A Handbook for Promoters* (Construction Research Communications for the Department of the Environment and Department of National Heritage, 1996).
Architectural Competitions: RIBA Code of Practice (RIBA, 1986).
Code of Practice for Fee Tendering (RIBA, 1991).

Notes

1 RIBA *Engaging an Architect: Guidance for Clients to Quality Based Selection* (RIBA, 1999).
2 O. Luder *A Guide to Keeping Out of Trouble* rev. and extended edn, p 21 (RIBA Publications, 2001).

6 Prerequisites to undertaking work

6.1 Competence and resources

Before accepting any commission, an architect – in the words of the *ARB Code of Professional Conduct and Practice,* Standard 1 – must be

> able to provide adequate professional, financial and technical competence and resources.

These requirements may be looked at in terms of type of building, size of commission and programme.

6.1.1 The type of building

In theory an architect can design any building type. This may be true given unlimited time for research, but the reality is that although most architects can design a wide range of non-specialist low-rise buildings of traditional construction, there can be real difficulties in undertaking a specialist building type with which one is not familiar. A practice that is regularly undertaking a specialist type of building is likely to be able to do it faster, with much less risk, and with knowledge of the latest innovations and legislation affecting the building type. Examples of such specialist building types might be process plants for the chemical, dying, leather and other industries, abattoirs, operating theatres, theme parks and large aquaria.

A practice with no experience in these or similar specialist fields will have to assess whether or not to take on the commission. If it decides to do so, it will need to assess how it is going to get the necessary expertise. This could be by allocating considerable time and personnel for research (which is likely to make the job unprofitable, and hence is applicable only if the commission is seen as one that will get the practice into a new sector); it could be by buying in the expertise from a practice that has it (which would probably mean working in conjunction with that practice on a shared fee basis); or it could be by recruiting a senior architect with the appropriate expertise (which is unlikely to be possible in the time available). Further assistance can be obtained by assembling a design team whose other members (quantity surveyor, structural engineer and services engineer) have wide experience in the particular specialist building type.

A similar situation arises when the proposed building is of non-traditional construction – for example a multistorey building of precast concrete panels. An ambitious and growing practice will not want to turn work away, but entering a new specialist field is likely to be a costly exercise. It is probably in the interests of the profession that practices do from time to time tackle new building types – otherwise no architects would ever enter new sectors – but they should only do so with their eyes open, and only after having made sure by careful assessments that the ARB Standard is going to be met.

6.1.2 The size of the commission

The situation is similar where the size of the building is outside the experience of the practice. For instance, for a small practice doing private housing to take on a 20-storey apartment block, or for a one-man band to take on a £25 million building, is to move into high-risk arenas. The work should either be turned down, or arrangements should be made to involve another practice or other practices, possibly on a joint-venture basis for a single project.

The available *human resources* always need serious consideration before accepting a commission:

- Who or which team is going to do it?
- How can this be fitted in with existing work?
- What is the programme that the client requires?
- Does it allow time to recruit staff?

6.1.3 Financial resources

The ARB Standard makes reference to financial resources. The usual problem is cash flow. If staff are taken on they have to be paid, and if the client requires extended credit, or is a slow payer, the situation can be desperate. A cash flow forecast is important for a large project.

Clients do from time to time go into liquidation or fall out with their architects, and thus every effort should be made to ensure that the client is not allowed to run up a large indebtedness to the practice.

In the case of every significant new commission a practice needs to ask itself 'Can the practice survive if the client fails?' If the answer is 'No', a very serious assessment of the client's financial standing needs to be undertaken, and the commission may be best left to others.

Bank loans taken out by architectural practices are likely to have to be backed by personal guarantees, and banks are notoriously fickle and prone to 'pull the rug'. There comes a point where the risks are unacceptable, and the practice may be better off without the commission.

6.1.4 The necessary technology

Increasingly clients require the architect to communicate documents and drawings by e-mail/Internet. The former may be relatively simple, the latter less so. The client and all the design team will need to ensure that their CAD systems are compatible. This area can have considerable cost implications and must be treated seriously.

6.1.5 Planning the handling of the project

In order to assess what fees to quote for a job, consideration will have to be given as to how it can be handled. This will be relatively easy if the project is similar to many that the practice have undertaken in recent years. It can be very difficult if the project is a one-off involving work of a type that is unfamiliar to the practice. In order to put a fee bid together, decisions often have to be made without the time required to go through textbook procedures. This is especially so where sub-consultants are involved. There will not be time for the detailed discussions and interviews that the commission really calls for, as the sub-consultancy team is likely to have to be put in place extremely quickly in order to formulate the response to the enquiry.

It is relatively easy when one has an established team that regularly works together. The situation is less simple when, for example, the building type is one in which the practice has limited expertise and it therefore wants to work with sub-consultants with a wealth of experience in the sector.

At fee bid stage the practice might well allocate its in-house team with a track record in the appropriate sector, but some caution is needed, because it may be some months before the labour-intensive production information stage is reached, by which time the chosen team may be fully committed on other work (or may have left!). The reserve team may take longer to do the work.

It is an unfortunate aspect of construction consultancy that practices, or departments within a practice, find it very difficult to regulate their workload. How often has one heard it said that it is either feast or famine? Experience indicates that many projects flounder en route or are delayed for a whole host of reasons, and a practice can be too cautious.

Example
A conscientious and competent practice turned down a very valuable commission because it did not believe that it could meet the timescale set by the client. Another practice took the commission, which was then delayed and came

to the production information stage just when the first practice needed such work. Its partners kicked themselves for years afterwards.

Techniques for coping with times of feast include:

- overtime working
- use of contract staff
- subcontracting parts of the work, e.g. design of drainage
- making maximum use of the design services of suppliers
- reusing relevant information from previous projects
- appointing other consultants who have worked with the practice on several occasions or on similar projects (or better still, both), who will deliver with minimum briefing, and are known to be supportive
- increasing quotations for less attractive clients or work
- turning away less attractive clients or work.

In times of famine a practice might:

- undertake work that might otherwise have been done by others, e.g. site surveys
- undertake clerk of works services in-house
- see if any clients would like perspectives or models (which can be done in-house)
- catch up on archiving
- undertake intensive marketing (but it may be too late!)
- undertake training
- produce standard details
- cut all overtime
- cut expenses
- dispense with contract staff
- go onto short-term working
- bring forward holidays
- take on work that in better times would be turned away
- reduce fee quotations
- set about 'site-finding' for clients
- undertake speculative work
- go in for competitions
- consider early retirements
- if all else fails make staff redundant: this must be done strictly within the law to avoid claims for wrongful dismissal, but at the same time a practice will not want to lose staff who are competent, reliable, hard-working, loyal and pleasant. Sadly there is a conflict between the humane desire to postpone redundancies as long as possible in the hope that work will materialise, and the commercial reality that staff with no fee-earning work to do cannot be carried in a harsh economic climate.

6.1.6 Quality assurance

The implementation of a quality assurance system may be of assistance in showing competence, and can be a useful marketing asset. Some clients demand it. It shows that systems are in place, but may give a false sense of security, for it is not in itself a guarantee of the adequacy of professional competence or adequate resources. Nevertheless it is often the better practices that are quality assured.

6.1.7 Quality of life

Architecture is a complex and challenging vocation. For some it will involve working as an employee, for others as a solo practitioner, or in a partnership or as a director of a practice. All leadership roles bring added stresses to an already stressful job. These include getting work, employing staff, cash flow, getting paid, and avoiding claims.

Anyone who does not have a robust temperament may do better not to take on these additional leadership roles; not all the stories of architects being driven insane or to an early grave by disastrous projects are apocryphal!

If an architect's clients and projects do not bring pleasure, job satisfaction and quality of life, it is better to plan for a change. Life is too short to be stuck in a job that brings only drudgery and stress. But for those who become masters of their calling, earn the respect of an established client list and design fine buildings or undertake allied consultancy work, whether as principal or employee, architecture, in spite of its generally poor remuneration, is a worthwhile vocation.

A practice that does not make profit is here today and gone tomorrow, but what value is profit unless partnered by quality of work and quality of life?

6.2 Professional indemnity insurance

Standard 7 of the *ARB Code of Professional Conduct and Practice* states:

> *Standard 7: An Architect should not undertake professional work without adequate and appropriate Professional Indemnity Insurance cover.*
>
> *7.1 The need for cover extends to professional work undertaken outside an Architect's main professional practice or employment.*
>
> *7.2 In the case of an employed Architect the Professional Indemnity Insurance cover may be provided by his Employer.*

The *RIBA Code of Professional Conduct* does not make professional indemnity insurance a prerequisite of undertaking work, but refers to a requirement to advise both employees and clients as follows:

Principle One

To uphold this Principle a Member undertakes:

1.2 When making any engagement, whether by an agreement for professional services, by a contract of employment or by a contract for the supply of services or goods, to state whether or not professional indemnity insurance is held, ...

And where professional indemnity insurance is held it must extend to employees:

Principle Three

To uphold this principle a Member undertakes:

3.11 To define the conditions of employment, authority, responsibility and liability of those Architects he employs, and ensure that any professional indemnity insurers waive their subrogation rights in respect of Members who are full-time employees.

SFA/99 and its derivatives, with the exception of SW/99, include the following:

7.4 The Architect shall maintain Professional Indemnity Insurance cover in the amount stated in the Appendix for any one occurrence or series of occurrences arising out of any one event until at least the expiry of the period stated in the Appendix from the date of the last Services performed under the Agreement or (if earlier) practical completion of the construction of the Project provided such insurance is available at commercially reasonable rates and generally available in the insurance market to the Architect.

The Architect, when requested by the Client, shall produce for inspection documentary evidence that the Professional Indemnity Insurance required under the Agreement is being maintained.

The Architect shall inform the Client if such insurance ceases to be available at commercially reasonable rates in order that the Architect and Client can discuss the best means of protecting their respective positions in respect of the project in the absence of such insurance.

The Appendix to the Conditions of SFA/99 includes a space to enter the *limit of liability and amount of Professional Indemnity Insurance cover,* and a footnote indicates that:

Unless otherwise stated, PII cover, excluding legal costs, will be not less than the amount required by the Architects Registration Board.

The *ARB Code of Professional Conduct and Practice* does not make reference to specific figures, but to adequate and appropriate cover.

Clause 7.4 is vitally important.

Example
Architects sued for outstanding fees of £8000 in connection with a nursing home extension. The client counterclaimed on the grounds that, owing to an initial survey error, rooms were too small, notwithstanding the fact that registration was achieved, and that window sills were too high to the extent that residents who were in bed or sitting in chairs could not see out of them. The counterclaim was circa £1.25 million. The court awarded damages of circa £500,000, which was the amount of the architects' insurance cover. Both sides appealed. The architects had not limited their liability, and practised as a partnership. Each partner faced the prospect of losing everything.

The ACA Standard Form of Contract for Project Partnering includes, inter alia, the following in connection with insurances:

19.4 Professional Indemnity Insurance or Product Liability Insurance shall be taken out by those Partnering Team Members and for those amounts stated against their names in the Project Partnering Agreement or any Joining Agreement, for the risks stated in Part 3 of Appendix 4, and shall be maintained throughout the limitation period referred to in Clause 27.8 unless such cover is no longer generally available in the market-place on reasonable terms and at reasonable premiums.

19.5 If so stated in the Commencement Agreement, Environmental Risk Insurance shall be taken out and maintained by the Partnering Team Member stated in the Commencement Agreement, in the amounts and for the risks and period stated in the Commencement Agreement.

19.6 If so stated in the Commencement Agreement, Latent Defects Insurance shall be taken out by the Partnering Team Member stated in the Commencement Agreement, in the amount and for the risks and period stated in the Commencement Agreement…

The Conditions of Appointment and Schedule of Services for Small Works (SW/99) is the exception, with no reference to professional indemnity insurance. SW/99 should not therefore be used where there can be any possibility that the architect's professional indemnity insurance limit may be exceeded unless a limit is set down in the appointment letter. It is remarkable how, once a dispute has commenced, sums escalate. Also, relatively modest projects can lead to huge consequential losses.

Examples

A small factory extension had a syphonic rainwater system. During a thunderstorm it failed and the factory flooded. Expensive electronic equipment was damaged, resulting in serious losses in production. The rainwater system had been designed by a specialist subcontractor, but there was no design warranty in place, no limitation of responsibility or limit of liability such as is given by SFA/99, and the subcontractor was no longer trading. The architect was not trading as a limited liability company. He was a worried man.

A church roof was re-slated. The detailing at the wall plate was less than satisfactory. The consequences, which only came to light many years later, were extensive outbreaks of dry rot. The cost of eradication was many times the cost of the original work.

Points to note in connection with indemnity insurance include the following:

- Cover must extend to every type of work that the practice is undertaking. There will be no problems in connection with basic architectural services; it is when unusual services are undertaken that the insurance may not apply. If in doubt the matter should be checked with insurers and the position confirmed in writing.
  Example. An architect had for many years undertaken extensions and alterations at a factory. A culvert ran beneath the grounds of the factory. The architect was asked to inspect it. Did his insurance extend to work of this type?
- Cover must extend to the wording of warranties. These are discussed in Chapter 8. It is unlikely that insurers will accept 'fitness for purpose' wording.
- Cover must extend to work undertaken by contract staff who may be employed by their own limited liability company and who are in effect labour-only subcontractors.
- Cover must extend to the work of sub-consultants, for which the architect will normally be responsible to the client. This will usually be by back-up cover in case the sub-consultants' insurance fails. It is vital to check the sub-consultants' insurances.
  Example. An architect provided architectural, structural engineering and quantity surveying services as a package. The structural engineering and quantity surveying was sub-let. The architect checked that both the subcontract practices had professional indemnity insurance. Several years later a structural problem came to light. By this time the consulting structural engineer had ceased trading. Was the architect covered for structural engineering work by

his own insurance? There may be a clause in the policy requiring notification to insurers where sub-consultants are engaged.

- Cover must extend to building survey work if this is undertaken. It may not, unless the work is undertaken by someone with a specified number of years' experience in this field, or there are exclusions in a specific form, for example: *The woodwork and other elements of the building which are covered, unexposed or inaccessible have not been inspected and no guarantee can be given as to their condition.*
  Such conditions can only be introduced before a contract is entered into. They are unlikely to stand up if merely written into the subsequent report. The Unfair Contract Terms Act 1977 may invalidate some exclusion clauses.
- Cover must extend to work undertaken by the partners or directors in a previous partnership or company. For example, if a practice has incorporated as a limited liability company, the professional indemnity insurance may not cover the previous partnership unless this is specifically referred to on the proposal form. Similarly, where two practices merge, the original practices may not be covered unless this is made clear on the proposal form.

Professional indemnity insurance is normally on the basis that insurers accept liability for claims notified during the period of insurance. Dangers here include:

- the failure to notify
  Example. Architects received a writ following the subsidence of a block of housing association flats. Insurers appointed solicitors, who made reassuring noises and borrowed the files. A few days later the solicitors wrote to the architects:
  We regret that a note on your file indicates that you were aware of a potential claim some two years ago, and we further regret that we must advise your insurers accordingly as the matter clearly arose before your present policy was effected. Thus it is unlikely that cover will extend to this present matter.
  The previous insurers did not want to know: their liability extended only to claims notified during their year of cover. In the interim the partner who had looked after the job had retired.
- notifications coming right at the end of a period of insurance.

From the above the following will be appreciated:

- the need for adequate professional indemnity insurance
- the need to understand the terms of that insurance and comply with them to the letter
- the risks of claims that for one reason or another are not covered by a practice's professional indemnity insurance, or which exceed the level of cover. Because this risk is not negligible, most prudent architects choose to practice with limited liability

- the importance of limiting liability, for example by SFA/99; but the limitation of liability in contract will rarely extend to claims in tort, which were referred to at the end of Chapter 1.

So far as warranties to third parties are concerned (discussed in Chapter 8), these need to limit the architect's liabilities to those set out in the contract with the architect's client.

All the SFA family of agreements exclude the rights of third parties in the following terms:

> *For the avoidance of doubt nothing in this Agreement shall confer or purport to confer on any third party any benefit or right to enforce any term of this Agreement.*

This limits the architect's responsibilities to the paying client and to any tortious claims. Any extension of responsibilities to third parties should be specifically spelt out, and the increased risks may need to be reflected in the fees charged.

The *Architect's Handbook of Practice Management* lists the eight areas that insurers have identified as the areas of highest risk:[1]

- taking over someone else's work (or vice versa) on a partial service basis
- structural-related surveys
- post-completion certification for building societies or other funders
- one-off houses built for non-NHBC-registered builders
- working for some housing associations
- design and build contracts, particularly those that do not limit design liability
- approving drawings by specialists and subcontractors
- acting as a sub-consultant without a proper appointing document.

Traditionally a solo practitioner might have chosen to save considerable professional indemnity insurance premiums by relying on a strong marriage and having all assets, and in particular his or her home, in the name of his or her spouse. Because of Standard 7 of the ARB Code of Professional Conduct and Practice, this is no longer possible.

Few architects are likely to sleep soundly with the horror of uninsured unlimited liability hanging over them.

6.3 Conflict

The ARB Code of Professional Conduct and Practice states at Standard 4:

4.2 An Architect should not accept or continue work if he has a business, financial or personal interest that is or may be in conflict with an interest of the client. In a borderline case the Architect should make full disclosure of an interest and leave it to the client to judge. However, some conflicts of interest are so extreme as to prevent the Architect entering into or continuing work, even with the client's knowledge and consent. Particular care is needed with respect to the business and commercial interests of any partners or co-directors of the Architect, which in this context are to be treated as his own.

4.3 Before agreeing to undertake work with two or more clients whose interests may be in conflict this fact should be made known to those concerned and, wherever possible, the work of the firm should be managed so as to avoid the interests of one client adversely affecting those of another. If it is not possible to disclose the existence of a conflict without a breach of confidence the Architect should decline to work for or disengage from work with one of the clients. He should not however act or continue to act for a client while in possession of relevant confidential information concerning another client or potential client.

The *RIBA Code of Professional Conduct* is even more verbose:

A Member shall, at all times, avoid any action of situation which is inconsistent with his professional obligations or which is likely to raise doubts about his integrity.

To uphold this Principle a Member undertakes:

2.1 To declare in writing to any prospective client or employer any business interest the existence of which, if not so declared, would or might be likely to raise a conflict of interests and doubts about his integrity by reason of an actual or apparent connection with or effect upon his engagement. If the prospective client or employer does not in writing accept these circumstances, the Member must withdraw from the situation.

2.2 When finding that in circumstances not specifically covered elsewhere in this Code his personal or professional interests conflict so as to risk a breach of this Principle either to withdraw from the situation, or remove the source of conflict, or declare it and obtain the agreement of the parties concerned to the continuance of the engagement.

2.3 Not in practice or purport to be an independent consulting Architect and simultaneously be a principal, partner, director or co-director in a firm which engages in the business of:
- *Trading in land or buildings; or as*
- *Property developers, auctioneers or house agents; or as*
- *Contractors, subcontractors, manufacturers or suppliers in or to the building industry*

unless that firm is distinct from the Architectural practice and clearly identified as such.

2.4 Not to carry out or purport to carry out the independent functions of an Architect or any similar independent functions in relation to a contract in which he or his employer is the Contractor, or where the Architectural practice and the Contractor's firm are under substantially the same management or control.

With different methods of working being explored, there is a temptation for some architects to change hats at some stage in a commission and put themselves in a position where there is likely to be a conflict of interest. Any such situation requires handling with the utmost care and integrity. Set out below are some cases where such care was not exercised and difficulties ensued. Any such changes must never be undertaken without a full explanation to the client of what is involved and the recommendation that the client take independent professional advice. This is not the case where the architect provides an extended consultancy role as a project manager or construction manager in a professional capacity.

Examples

The shell of a building was procured along the traditional route with separate architect and contractor. The same contractor was then engaged on a design and build basis to do the fit out and employed the same architect as sub-consultant. A JCT Minor Works form was incorrectly used for the design and build contract, leaving the sub-consultant architect to certify monies from his original employer to his new employer, the builder. The architect should not have put himself in the position where he was certifying the work, and should have flagged up that the form of contract was not appropriate.

An architect undertook to provide a construction management service for an extension on a percentage fee. The employer was told that this would save the builder's overheads and profit, and that the employer would pay only what the building cost. The building cost very significantly more than the budget. The architect turned out to be the owner of the building company that was used.

An architect designed a major leisure facility. The architect also had a building company, and the employer was impressed by the products of that company. After approvals had been obtained in the traditional manner, the architect's building company was appointed on a design and build basis. The employer appointed his maintenance man, who had never seen a JCT contract, as employer's agent. The architect drew up the Employer's Requirements. All went well until the employer ran out of money and the design and build contractor sued. As is not unusual when an employer is sued, a team of experts was engaged to rake through the building with a toothcomb to set up a counterclaim.

The expert engineer said the structure was flawed and the building would have to be taken down. The architect, whose original commission as designer had never been terminated, was now also the contractor's MD. The counterclaim was against the builder and the architect. It was argued that the employer had relied on the architect's advice throughout.

An architect acted as Employer's Agent under a design and build contract. Subsequently he also acted for the contractor, without ceasing to be the Employer's Agent. Inevitably there was conflict. The project ended in arbitration.

A delicate area is when to advise the client to take legal advice in non-contentious circumstances. For example, in a complicated contract there may be merit in involving a non-contentious construction lawyer in the drafting of the contract, but is the lawyer then going to also draft unacceptable terms of engagement for the architect? The answer, if possible, is to get the architect's agreement signed first.

Further reading

*ARB Code of Professional Conduct and Practice (Architects' Registration Board, 1997).
A. Burns (ed.) The Legal Obligations of the Architect (Butterworth, 1994).
*D. Chappell and A. Willis, A. The Architect in Practice 8th edn, Chapters 2, 16 and 17 (Blackwell Science, 2000).
D.L. Cornes Design Liability in the Construction Industry 4th edn (Blackwell, 1994).
*S. Cox and A. Hamilton Architect's Handbook of Practice Management 6th edn, Chapters A4, B3 and F4 (RIBA Publications, 1998).
A. Lavers and D. Chappell A Legal Guide to the Professional Liability of Architects 3rd edn (RIBA Publications, 2000).
*F.A. Paterson Professional Indemnity Insurance Explained (RIBA Publications, 1995).
*Code of Professional Conduct and Standard of Professional Performance (RIBA Publications, 1997).
*Architects Continuing Professional Development Requirements and Guidance Notes for Members (RIBA, 1999).
M. Taylor Avoiding Claims in Building Design: Risk Management in Practice (Blackwell Science, 2000).

Note

1 p 215.

7 Procurement methods

The procurement method to be adopted has a profound effect on the services required from the architect, and hence the terms of engagement and fees. In many projects the architect will be expected to give advice on the procurement method. For both these reasons it is important for architects to have at least a basic knowledge of the main methods of procurement. Cox and Clamp, in the second edition of *Which Contract?*, refer to a *contract profile* involving the conflicting criteria of cost, time and quality. They then compare the basic procurement methods in terms of speed, complexity, quality, flexibility, certainty, competition, responsibility and risk.

7.1 Traditional procurement

7.1.1 JCT98, IFC98 and MW98

Here the architect designs the building, prepares the production information, obtains prices by tender or negotiation, and administers the building contract. RIBA forms of appointment SFA/99, CE/99 and SW/99 all relate to this procurement method, and refer back to the RIBA Plan of Work. The fundamental characteristic is that the responsibilities for design and construction are vested in two separate organisations: the *design team* and the *contractor*.

Provided the design has been fully developed before tenders are invited, tendering costs are minimised and proper competition is ensured, the final project costs will be lower than when using most other procurement methods, and there is a higher degree of certainty that the required standards of quality and function will be met than with other procurement systems. On the other hand, because the design needs to be fully developed, this method may take longer in the design stage, and also, because of the contractor's lack of input during the design stage, the 'buildability' may not have had the fullest consideration. Furthermore, although the existence of a priced bill of quantities enables interim valuations to be assessed easily and variations to be priced quickly, the employer is likely to pay heavily for any delays caused by, and disruptive effects of, variations. Overall this remains the best procurement method for many buildings, but they do need to be fully designed pre-tender.

There are a number of variants on traditional procurement, including those described below.

7.1.2 Two-stage selective tendering

This method may be appropriate when speed of completion assumes more importance than cost but cost nevertheless remains important. An approximate bill of quantities is prepared, or even notional quantities or a schedule of rates, based on preliminary drawings. A small number of contractors tender on the basis of these documents while the more detailed drawings are being prepared. The successful tenderer will then work with the design team on the understanding that parties will enter into a contract at a figure based upon total re-measurement of the project once working drawings are available. By agreement, early orders can be placed for critical elements. The fact that additional costs are likely to be incurred must be balanced against the advantage that completion will normally be achieved earlier then when using the full traditional procurement system. Because work is likely to be commenced before a final tender sum is agreed, early price certainty needs to be a secondary consideration.[1]

7.1.3 Negotiated contracts

This system allows the contractor to be chosen at a very early stage on the basis of expertise and proven track record, and the PQS (that is, the private or professional quantity surveyor) will negotiate rates and the overall tender price with the contractor's QS. Alternatively, the negotiations may be based on a priced bill for a similar project won by the contractor in competition.

This approach has many advantages, not least the opportunity to work with a contractor chosen because of proven management and quality, and whose approach to claims is fair and reasonable. There is also the advantage of having the builder on the team at design stage to give input on construction methods. Negotiated contracts may be expected to show a modest reduction in time; quality is likely to be high but there is likely to be a cost premium of perhaps 5%, although in fact there may well be a hidden cost benefit to the employer as a result of the input of the contractor's commercial expertise during the design stage coupled with the probable reduction in claims.

Negotiated contracts are particularly appropriate when there are specific circumstances – if, for example:

- an immediate start has to be made
- the work is of a specialist or unusual nature and the chosen contractor has the expertise to do it.

But negotiated contracts do not need to be restricted to these circumstances, and this is a very good procurement method in many situations.

It is important for public bodies to show that their procurement methods are above board and that contracts have not been handed out on the 'old boy network' or in some other manner totally inappropriate to a public body. Thus negotiated contracts may not be appropriate for a public body, and any such body using them should protect itself by:

- holding formal interviews with several possible contractors, probably with some outside independent assistance, in order to select the appropriate contractor
- obtaining a formal report from an independent quantity surveyor that the negotiated figure is a fair one and recommending its acceptance.

7.1.4   Continuity or serial contracts

Where an employer has a number of building projects, generally of a similar type and in the same geographical area, there can be considerable advantages in continuity contracts, whereby it is understood that the successful contractor on the first project will be awarded subsequent contracts on a negotiated basis subject to satisfactory performance; or a number of serial contracts are tendered for on a master bill of quantities. The potential advantages are obvious, with close cooperation between employer, design team and contractor leading in most cases to improved performance, reduced cost and reduced time.

7.1.5   Cost-reimbursable contracts

Variants include *cost plus* contracts and *target cost* contracts. Under the cost plus contract the contractor is reimbursed for the actual cost of the works plus a fee to cover overheads and profit. In target cost contracts a target cost is agreed for the work, together with a fee to cover the contractor's overheads, management and profit, and a mechanism is agreed for sharing any savings or additions if the actual cost is lower or higher than the target cost.

The absence of cost control makes this approach appropriate only in rare cases, such as when taking over a project following the bankruptcy of the original contractor, or in the event of fire, storm or flood damage where significant ongoing consequential losses make speed all important. This type of contract is also applicable where the scope of the works cannot readily be defined at tender stage – possibly, for example, in the eradication of dry rot or in some conservation work.

7.1.6 Standard forms of contract for traditional procurement

The main standard forms of building contract for traditional procurement are:

- the *standard lump sum forms:*
  - JCT Standard Form of Building Contract 1998 Edition (JCT98)
  - the ACA Form of Building Agreement 3rd edn (1998)
  - GC/Works 1 with Quantities (1998)
  - the Engineering and Construction Contract 2nd edn.
- the *shorter lump sum forms:*
  - JCT Intermediate Form of Building Contract for works of simple content 1998 Edition (IFC98)
  - JCT Agreement for Minor Building Works (1998 edn) (MW98)
  - GC/Works/2 (1998)
  - JCT Standard Form of Tender and JCT Agreement for Building Works of a Jobbing Character JA/T90 (used with Conditions of Contract for Building Works of a Jobbing Nature JA/C90)
  - JCT Agreement for Renovation Grant Works
  - ASI forms of contract.
- *measurement forms:*
  - JCT Standard Form of Building Contract 1998 Edition with Approximate Quantities
  - JCT Standard Form of Measured Terms Contract (1998)
  - ICE Conditions of Contract 6th edn
  - ICE Conditions of Contract, Minor Works 2nd edn.
- *cost plus forms:*
  - JCT Standard Form of Prime Cost Contract (1998).

Details of the up-to-date editions of all the main standard forms and amendments are helpfully set out in the annual list of RIBA Publications.

7.2 Design and build

7.2.1 WCD98 and CDPS98

A significant proportion of building work is undertaken on a *design and build* basis. The key feature is a single point of contact between employer and contractor, with the contractor taking responsibility for both the design and the construction of the project. This may give advantages in time and cost, and may be advantageous to the employer if the building turns out to be seriously defective. On the other hand it is likely to be more difficult for the employer to get the building they need and the quality they want.

A design and build contract will have an implied standard of *fitness for purpose* unless there is a specific alternative written into the contract, as there is, for example, in WCD98, where the standard form places on the contractor the same design responsibility as that *of an architect:* that is, with the responsibility to use reasonable skill and care, rather than having an absolute liability.

There are three roles in a design and build contract that may be undertaken by architects:

- preparation of the Employer's Requirements
- acting as the Employer's Agent
- preparation of the Contractor's Proposals and acting as the contractor's architect.

Logically the first two should go together, and an entirely different architect should prepare the Contractor's Proposals and act as the contractor's architect.

It will be appreciated that there are difficulties with design and build contracts so far as planning permission is concerned, and the employer is faced with one of the following options:

- To arrange for the Employer's Requirements to include designs, possibly detailed designs, for which planning permission has already been obtained prior to inviting design and build tenders. Given a detailed design, coupled with a specification of the required standards of finishes etc., there may not be a lot left for the design and build contractor to design.
- To proceed by way of a two-stage tender, with a considerable delay while the successful stage 1 tenderer seeks to obtain planning permission before the main design and build contract can be entered into.

It is vital for an architect engaged by the employer in a design and build situation to agree with his client which of the above approaches is preferred, as the work required will be very different. The former may involve the architect having to undertake a lot of design work, whereas the latter is more likely to involve the preparation of a schedule of requirements and performance data.

Design and build will work satisfactorily only when the Employer's Requirements are very carefully prepared. When the employer does not have a skilled design team to prepare the requirements and to evaluate the contractors' submissions, then the design and build procurement system is likely to end in disaster. The fact that many employers do not appreciate this is the main reason why there have been so many criticisms of design and build.

In preparing the Employer's Requirements the architect will almost certainly need assistance from M & E engineers and probably from a structural engineer. For an employer who has not undertaken a design and build project before, the architect may have to undertake quite a lot of client education.

It is entirely appropriate that the lead consultant who has prepared the Employer's Requirements should act as the Employer's Agent under the JCT Standard Form of Contract With Contractor's Design 1998 (WCD98), which is becoming the norm for design and build projects.

Where the Employer's Requirements include a well-advanced design, the employer, wishing to ensure that the contractor is fully responsible for that design, may seek to novate the architect to the contractor. Novation and its half-sister *consultant switch* are discussed in Chapter 14. They are less than ideal.

The work required of the contractor's architect will be largely dependent on the nature of the Employer's Requirements. If these are in the form of a performance specification, there really will be design competition, with a lot of work for the architect. If, however, the Employer's Requirements already include detailed designs, there may be very little for the contractor's architect to do, and possibly nothing at tender stage.

The RIBA has published an amendment to SFA/99 and CE/99 entitled *Amendment for Procurement of Employers Requirements for a Design and Build Contract* (DB1/99). The notes in this document include the following:

> In the Pre-Construction phase the Architect may provide services in any or all of Work Stages A–F prior to completing development of the 'Employer's Requirement' document by way of prescriptive information or performance specification at Stage G and inviting tenders at stage H. Carefully consider which activities in the Services Supplement to this Amendment are necessary to identify and allocate risks between Client and Contractor.

It also includes the following note:

> Use of DB1/99 where Consultant Switch is contemplated.

> SFA/99 with this Amendment should be used for the initial appointment of the Architect where the Client and the Architect agree that the Contractor is to enter into an Agreement with the Architect for the preparation of the Contractor's Proposals....

> The Agreement should include an additional recital foreshadowing a Tripartite Agreement between Client, Contractor and Architect.

There is a second amendment to SFA/99 entitled *Amendment where the Client is the*

Contractor under a Design and Build Contract (DB2/99). It includes notes advising as follows:

> *This Amendment is suitable for use with SFA/99 where an Architect is appointed by the Contractor to prepare Contractor's Proposals for a building project to be procured under the JCT Standard Form of Building Contract with Contractor's Design (WCD98) or the JCT with Contractor's Designed Portion Supplement (CDPS98).*

> *The modifications to the Conditions or to the Architect's activities in performing the Services set out in this Amendment can be tailored to suit the requirements of the Contractor Client and the Project.*

> *Note that the special work stages for Contractor's Proposals relevant to the Services and their timing will be dependent on the extent on which the Contractor Client or the Employer's Requirements and/or the tender invitation require the design and constructional detail to be developed at tender stage.*

> *It will be noted that although submission of the Project for detailed Development Control Approval is indicated at Stage D, other statutory or other approvals are deferred until acceptance of the Contractor's tender at Stage J: Mobilisation.*

Once the contract is let, the role of the architect as Employer's Agent is defined in DB1/99 to include the following:

> *The Architect has authority and responsibility in the tender and construction Work Stages H–L for:*

> *1 Inviting and appraising a tender or tenders including:*
> *— considering with the Client a tenderer or a list of tenderers for the works*
> *— coordinating review of recommended Contractor's Proposals*
> *— considering with the Client appointment of a Contractor and the responsibilities of the parties and the Employer's Agent under the building contract*
> *— preparing a building contract and arranging for signatures*

> *2 Administering the building contract as agent of the Employer, including:*
> *— monitoring the progress of the Works against the Contractor's programme*
> *— coordinating review of further Contractor's Proposals*
> *— issuing information, instructions, etc.*
> *— preparing valuations of work carried out or completed and preparing financial reports for Client*
> *— advising the Client on valuations of work prepared by others, and presenting financial reports prepared by others to Client*
> *— collating record information including for the Health and Safety File*

3 Coordinating and monitoring the work of Consultants and Site Inspectors, if any, to the extent required for the administration of the building contract, including:...

Key points for the Employer's Agent to watch are as follows:

- To what extent is he or she responsible for site inspection, particularly bearing in mind that most architects and building clerks of works are not qualified to inspect complex services installations?
- On what basis is the contractor to submit interim valuations? The easiest way is usually on the basis of lump sums against each element completed. If the valuations are to be on the basis of the actual work done on site, the employer will need to engage a quantity surveyor, either directly or as sub-consultant to the Employer's Agent.
- What will be the position if the contractor goes into liquidation? The Employer's Agent needs to ensure that he or she has not allowed the employer to have paid for work that is incomplete or defective; nor to have accepted a front-loaded payment schedule.

7.2.2 System building

There are various system buildings on the market that enable an employer to buy a building, often quite sophisticated, built from standard components put together to suit the client's requirements. The client is usually able to see actual examples of such buildings before purchasing them. WCD98 may be an appropriate contract to use for such buildings. The architect as Employer's Agent may deal with the planning authority and liase with the contractor about the layout, but it is unlikely that the architect's work will be extensive.

7.2.3 PFI projects

The PFI contractor is responsible not only for the design and construction of the building, but also for financing it and for the subsequent facilities management over perhaps a 25-year term. The PFI contractor may be a major contractor or developer or, probably more likely, a consortium. The form of contract will be bespoke. Appropriate documents to form the basis for the architect's engagement by the consortium or contractor are SFA/99, perhaps with amendment DB2/99.

7.2.4 Turnkey projects

Turnkey projects are particularly found in heavy engineering, where the civil engineering work is subservient to the mechanical engineering and the machinery manufacturer is the main contractor: for example power stations, petrochemical plants or refuse treatment works. The architect, consulting civil engineer and builder are all likely to be in a subcontract role. SFA/99 is appropriate. An important point to watch is that, as with PFI contracts, the main contract will not normally be the JCT contract with which architects are familiar, and they should avoid signing up to something that gives them a liability beyond the bounds of their PI insurance cover.

7.2.5 Standard forms of contract for design and build procurement

The main standard forms of contract for full or partial design and build procurement are:

- JCT Standard Form of Building Contract With Contractor's Design, 1998 Edition (WCD98)
- JCT Standard Form of Building Contract With Quantities, 1998 Edition With Contractor's Designed Portion Supplement
- ICE Design and Construct Conditions of Contract
- GC/Works/1 Single Stage Design and Build (1998)
- The ACA Forms of Building Agreement (3rd edn, 1998).

7.3 Management contracting

The main characteristics for this procurement system include the following:

- The design team is appointed by the employer.
- The contractor is appointed, following interviews and possibly tenders, on a professional basis in a similar manner to the members of the design team.
- The contractor is reimbursed on the basis of a lump sum or percentage fee for management services in addition to the actual cost of construction.
- The actual construction is carried out by works package contractors, who are employed as subcontractors to, and coordinated and administered by, the management contractor.
- Subcontractors must be financially independent from the management contractor.

There is a JCT Standard Form of Management Contract, published in 1987, revised 1998, together with a suite of related documents. The practice note relating to this contract indicates that the usual arrangement is for the client to appoint the design consultants in advance of the engagement of the management contractor and to be responsible for their reimbursement and management. They then prepare the initial designs, invite tenders from management contractors, and advise on their appointment. SFA/99 will possibly be appropriate.

An alternative approach is for the management contractor to be engaged in advance of the architect and other consultants and made responsible for their appointments and for the reimbursement of the design team, in which case SFA/99 with DB2/99 will probably be appropriate.

Various criticisms of this form of procurement have been identified[2] that have led to clients' 'disenchantment' with it, including:

- delays caused by trade/package contractors over which the client has no control
- the additional costs of procurement using this system, which, it is suggested, may on average be 12% more than those of other procurement methods
- the difficulties experienced in achieving reasonable quality standards
- the limitation of the contractor's liabilities to those arising from negligence in the performance of his management function
- the allocation of the majority of the project risks to the client – this can be particularly onerous where works-package contractors fail to perform and affect the following and parallel works-package contractors
- an increase in the amount of administrative effort and paperwork required.

Example

A works-package contractor was engaged to apply a specialist finish to plastered walls in a high-tech environment. The finish failed to the extent that it needed to be replaced. Unfortunately it could not be removed without damaging the plaster, to the extent that the plaster had to be removed. Other works-package contractors, notably the mechanical and electrical, were severely disrupted and delayed. The defaulting contractor went into liquidation. There was no negligence on the part of the management contractor. It cost the client a lot of money.

Set against this is the primary advantage of this system that it enables commencement of the project on site to be accelerated, which in turn should lead to earlier completion; also, it may limit the financial penalties of late variations.

A variant is management contracting with a guaranteed maximum price, but it may be argued that this will compromise the contractor's status as the client's advisor.

7.4 Construction management

The main characteristics of this system of procurement include the following:

- The construction manager is appointed as a consultant at an early stage along with, and having a similar status to, the members of the design team.

- Payment of the construction manager is by means of a lump sum or percentage fee for management services.
- The actual construction of the project is carried out by works package contractors who are employed by the client but coordinated, supervised and administrated by the construction manager, who also coordinates the other consultants.

As a variant the design team may also be engaged on behalf of the employer, in the same manner as works contractors, by the construction manager. In any event SFA/99 is appropriate.

Construction managers may agree a fee structure with the client that will incorporate cost penalties and incentives that can be applied if the agreed criteria are, or are not, achieved.

There is no reason why an architect should not provide construction management services, although only a few practices have the necessary experience to manage complex construction projects. Such practices will be aware of the need for appropriate terms of engagement.

For the employer, construction management has similar advantages and disadvantages to management contracting.

7.5 The BPF hybrid

This system, introduced by the British Property Federation in the 1980s, involves:

- a very important client's representative, who is responsible for the contract from concept to completion
- a design leader, and other consultants, appointed on lump sum fees for each stage, with the possibility of being awarded a supplementary payment if the design work is completed on time and the design is within budget. However, the design team does not design everything, and the specification includes items that have not been designed by the design team, but are left to the contractor: limits are specified within which these remaining elements are to designed
- a supervisor to assist the client's representative when the project is on site.

Appropriate forms of contract are the ACA form specially prepared for use with this procurement system or JCT with Contractor's Designed Portion Supplement.

So far as the architect is concerned, the extent of the design work required must be specified in order to be priced. Subject to this, SFA/99 is appropriate.

An architect may also be engaged by the contractor to assist in the design in those elements that are left to the contractor, in which case SFA/99 with DB2/99 is likely to be appropriate.

7.6 Partnering

Baden Hellard opens his book *Project Partnering* with the bold statement

> The 'partnering' philosophy is the master key that will unlock the techniques and principles of TQM [total quality management] to provide customer satisfaction on construction projects. [3]

Partnering is a current buzzword. In many ways it is taking construction back to where it was 50 years ago – and a lot healthier it was then, when architects, contractors and subcontractors who knew each other often worked together as fairly regular teams, generally in quite small geographical areas.

Will 21st century partnering work? The probability is that it will, because of the very considerable effort that the system puts into choosing the partners, as poignantly illustrated by Baden Hellard, who refers to in-depth third-party auditing visits to prospective partners to examine and discuss:

- examples of previous and current work by the company
- the likely management structure for the project
- examples of documents and contract methods for other projects
- methods of cost control, together with methods for dealing with deviations
- procedures for maintaining and improving quality standards.

If this care is taken in appointing the key players in a project it is likely that the project will be successful. As experienced construction professionals know, project successes and disasters are much more likely to be traceable back to relationships on site than to a particular form of procurement. A project having a good team with, in the current jargon, a 'win/win and get it right first time' mentality is likely to succeed. A project with a poor or badly remunerated team is likely to be a failure. Partnering's emphasis on careful choice of partners, increased communication between the key players and the probability that most will want to be involved in the next partnering scheme, augur well for the system. But, as with a negotiated contract, the probability is that it will cost the client more, despite the 'open book' approach all round, but this may be offset by a reduction in claims.

To date the main form of contract for partnering is the ACA Standard Form of Contract for Project Partnering known as PPC 2000. This is not a stand-alone document so far as consultants are concerned, but is supplemented by a consultant services schedule for each client-appointed consultant, together with agreed consultant payment terms.

As with any other arrangement, the architect needs to take care not to make a commitment to any terms or conditions that are unacceptable, and that the responsibilities to the contractor (known in the ACA form as *the Constructor*) are not incompatible with the responsibilities to the client.

Partnering is not a panacea for all ills. There have already been disasters in demonstration projects that were selected to show the advantages of partnering by those who promote partnering. Partnering contracts where a partner or partners start to lose money are likely to become as sour and adversarial as any other contracts where that happens. A construction lawyer has written the following on this topic:[4]

> *The drawbacks of a partnering approach are that, like marriages, relationships deteriorate. Then there is the argument that a contract based on good faith alone is imparting something that English law doesn't recognise. There are obvious limitations about confirming partnering agreements. Measuring 'best value' will also provide its own challenges.*

But the article concludes:

> *. . . genuinely using partnering to re-jig your relationships one to another, provides real opportunities despite the drawbacks.*

Indeed any practice that can get into a good partnering contract on reasonable terms is likely to benefit considerably from doing so. It should, however, be cautious. An expression of intention to cooperate may have the undesired effect of diluting specific contractual terms in the agreement: a non-binding expression of cooperation may give rise to unintended legal consequences.[5]

In building procurement it remains as true today as when John Ruskin wrote it that:

> *There is hardly anything in the world today that someone cannot make just a little worse and sell a little cheaper and people who buy on price alone are this man's lawful prey.*

Further reading

R. Baden Hellard *Project Partnering: Principle and Practice* (Thomas Telford, 1995).

BPF *Manual of the BPF System: The British Property Federation System for Building Design and Construction* (British Property Federation, 1983).

D. Brown *After the Divorce – Problems with Partnering Agreements* (Society of Construction Law, 2001).

*D. Chappell and A. Willis *The Architect in Practice* 8th edn, Chapter 7 (Blackwell Science, 2000).

CIC *Project Partnering Guide* (CIC, 2000).

*S. Cox and A. Clamp *Which Contract? Choosing the Appropriate Building Contract* 2nd edn (RIBA Publications, 1999).

J. Franks *Building Procurement Systems: A Client's Guide* 3rd edn (Longmans, 1998).

J. Hackett *Design and Build: Uses and Abuses* (LLP, 1998).

JCT with Building Design Partnership *The JCT Guide to the Use of Performance Specifications* (RIBA Publications, 2001).

HM Treasury *Step by Step Guide to the PFI Procurement Process* rev. edn (HM Treasury, 1999).

JCT Practice Note No. 4 (Series 2): Partnering (2001).

M. Lenihan and J. Redmond *To 'B' or 'D & B'? Design and Build in the 90s* (Society of Construction Law, 1994).

*J.W.E. Masterman *An Introduction to Building Procurement Systems* (E & FN Spon, 1992).

*D. Mosey *Design and Build in Action* (Chandos, 1998).

D. Mosey *PPC 2000: The First Standard Form of Contract for Project Partnering* (Society of Construction Law, 2001).

R. Moxley *Building Management by Professionals* (Butterworth Architecture, 1993).

NJCC *Code of Procedure for Two Stage Selective Tendering* (NJCC, 1996).

NJCC *Code of Practice for Selective Tendering for Design and Build* (NJCC, 1996).

*RIBA Publications *Annual List of Publications*.

Notes

1 NJCC *Code of Procedure for Two Stage Selective Tendering* (NJCC, 1996).

2 J.W.E. Masterman *An Introduction to Building Procurement Systems* Chapter 5 (E & FN Spon, 1992).

3 R. Baden Hellard *Project Partnering: Principle and Practice* Chapter 4 and Appendix 1 (Thomas Telford, 1995).

4 Anthony Glaister, office factsheet, Keeble Hawson, 2001.

5 *Birse Construction Ltd v St David Ltd* [1999] BLR194.

8 Warranties to third parties

Recent decades have seen a reduction in the tortious responsibility, as opposed to contractual responsibility, of one party to another in construction projects. This has led to the widespread use of warranties that create a contractual link between the parties who enter into them, and are capable of being assigned to other parties.

Thus nominated subcontractors under JCT80 or named subcontractors under IFC98 who undertake specialist design work will be expected to give warranties in favour of the employer. It is important to the architect that these warranties are in place as, if the subcontractor's design fails and they are not in place, the architect may find him or herself in difficulties.

Similarly if a party who purchases a completed development wants to have rights of recovery against consultants, contractor and subcontractors who undertook defective design and construction, it will be necessary to obtain warranties from the designers and contractors.

In the case of management contracting, the employer may require warranties from all the works package subcontractors. A purchaser acquiring a development built by way of construction management may require warranties from every trade contractor. In a design and build contract the employer may require warranties from the design team, possibly as a 'belt and braces' arrangement to give some protection in case the contractor goes into liquidation. An architect may be asked to give warranties to all sorts of people, including prospective purchasers or tenants or financiers.

A standard form of warranty to be given by consultants to financiers has been agreed between the BPF, the RIBA, ACE and the RICS.

Occupiers are likely to want warranties, be they purchasers of completed buildings or tenants with repairing obligations. It is usual for warranties to be granted that are assignable to first purchasers and first tenants only.

In deciding whether or not an architect is under a legal obligation to give a warranty, the first question to ask is, 'Has a contract with the client been concluded?' If it has, does that contract include a commitment to provide warranties and, if it does, to whom and in what form?

Vital points for the architect to note include the following:

- The warranty must be time related and not open ended: thus, for example, for 6 years from practical completion.
- Warranties that include the right to pass them on to others in an unending daisy chain are to be avoided.
- The architect must not warrant to a third party obligations beyond those owed to the client. This calls for wording such as:
  The Architect shall have no duties or obligations to the Purchaser which are greater than he owes to the Client under the Appointment.
- The warranty should not go beyond reasonable skill and care. A clause such as the following is appropriate:
  The Architect warrants that he has exercised reasonable skill and care in the performance of his duties and obligations under the Appointment.

If a warranty includes a fitness for purpose clause, the result is to impose a higher standard of care on the architect than the usual standard for a professional person of reasonable skill and care, and it should not be accepted. Fitness for purpose imposes an obligation to achieve a particular result, and if the architect fails in this he or she will be liable, regardless of fault. In a case of reasonable skill and care it is a defence to show that the architect did not fall below the standard prevailing in the profession at the time the work was undertaken. The architect needs to avoid such disguised fitness for purpose clauses as:

The Architect warrants and undertakes to the purchaser that the design of the development will in all respects meet the stated requirements of the client.

Most professional indemnity insurance policies do not cover fitness for purpose obligations.

Similarly most professional indemnity insurance policies will not cover liabilities arising from an indemnity that increases the scope of recoverable loss beyond that normally recovered for a breach of contract, and care must be taken that any warranty does not extend the limitation period.

If the architect is giving a warranty it is important to ensure that other parties who might also be responsible should give warranties. For example, it would be inequitable for the architect to be giving a warranty if the contractor did not do so, as it is more likely that problems will arise from the contractor's workmanship than from the architect's design.

As with contracts, warranties can be executed under hand and be enforceable for six years, or be signed as a deed and be enforceable for 12 years. But note that these periods of time run from the date the warranties become operative and not from the dates they are signed.

Example

An architect entered into a design warranty, as a deed, in favour of the first purchaser of the building, but the client put tenants in and did not sell it for 12 years, leaving the architect with liabilities for 24 years.

Architects should expect to be paid for warranties because they are likely to seriously extend the classes of people to whom liability will be owed.

It may be that the Contracts (Rights of Third Parties) Act 1999 will reduce the reliance on warranties, but for the moment they are with us, and architects need to be very cautious both in ensuring that the employer has warranties from subcontractors who undertake design work and in ensuring that the architect does not enter into any warranties that extend his or her liabilities, in either scope or time, beyond those owed to the client.

The Contracts (Rights of Third Parties) Act 1999 provides that where a term of a contract confers a right on a person who is not a party to that contract, the party has the right to enforce that term. It is possible to exclude this right, and all standard forms of appointment published by the RIBA contain an exclusion clause to prevent third parties from bringing claims against the architect. Architects should ensure that an exclusion clause is included in any non-standard terms they agree to. Notwithstanding such an exclusion clause, an architect could still be joined into an action as a third party in litigation in the courts.

Example

A tenant fell downstairs and sued the landlord housing association on the grounds of a design fault in the stairs; the housing association joined in the architect as a third party.

Further reading

BPF *Form of Agreement for Collateral Warranty to be Given by Consultant in Favour of Funding Institution* 3rd edn (British Property Federation, 1992).

BPF *Form of Agreement for Collateral Warranty to be Given by Consultant in favour of Purchaser or Tenant* 2nd edn (British Property Federation, 1993).

D.L. Cornes and R. Winward *Collateral Warranties: A Practical Guide for the Construction Industry* (BSP, 1990).

NJCC *Guidance Note 6: Collateral Warranties* (NJCC, 1992).

F.A. Paterson *Collateral Warranties Explained* (RIBA Publications, 1991).

9   The need for written terms of engagement and the use of standard forms of agreement

The ARB Code of Professional Conduct and Practice includes at Standard 4:

4.1 An Architect should not undertake work unless the parties have clearly agreed in writing the terms of the contract notably as to:

- *the scope of the works*
- *the allocation of responsibilities*
- *any limitation of responsibilities*
- *the fee or method of calculation of it; and*
- *any provision for termination*

The RIBA Code of Professional Conduct states at 1.2:

When making any engagement, whether by an agreement for professional services, by a contract of employment or by a contract for the supply of services and goods, to state whether or not professional indemnity insurance is held, and to have defined beyond reasonable doubt and recorded the terms of the engagement and the scope of the service, responsibilities and any limitation of liability, the method of calculation of remuneration and the provision for termination and adjudication.

Thus it is a disciplinary offence under both ARB and the RIBA for an architect to undertake work without a written agreement.

The foreword to the RIBA publication *A Client's Guide to Engaging an Architect Including Guidance on Fees* states:[1]

It is no exaggeration to say that a major part of the work of any lawyer practising in the construction industry consists of trying to ascertain what really are the contractual intentions of parties who have not found the time to document the relationship properly.

It is no coincidence that both the RIBA and the ARB Codes of Professional Conduct stress the need for a formal record of the terms of the Architect's Engagement by the Client. The new forms are the result of much effort on the part of their authors not only to bring them in line with current legislation, but also to make them more user-friendly than before.

The new forms referred to are each considered briefly below. It is of course entirely feasible for architect and client to set out their contractual arrangements by an exchange of letters, or for a practice to have its own in-house terms of engagement, or for a bespoke contract to be drawn up for the engagement of the architect.

A lot of effort has gone into the preparation of the RIBA forms, which are published in association with the Royal Incorporation of Architects in Scotland, the Royal Society of Ulster Architects and the Association of Consultant Architects. They protect both architect and client, not least by spelling out exactly where each stands. Some of the provisions may, however, fall foul of the Unfair Contract Terms Act 1977 under certain circumstances.

Where contracts are entered into under hand, there is a liability for six years (see Chapter 1). This will normally be from the date of practical completion unless the period was re-started later, for example by the architect's giving further advice. Where the contract is executed as a deed the liability is for 12 years. In addition there may be a tortious liability, initially for six years and thereafter within three years of the claimant's having knowledge of the complaint, normally with a longstop of 15 years. An ill-considered form of warranty may give rise to a liability for a period longer than 15 years.

Each of the RIBA's standard forms comprises:

- conditions, intended to be taken as standard
- schedules for recording the requirements, the services to be provided, fees and expenses, and the appointment of other consultants, specialists or site staff
- articles of agreement for recording the essential details of the agreement reached – alternatively some forms are used with a letter of appointment.

9.1 Standard Form of Agreement for the Appointment of an Architect (SFA/99)

This form is for use where an architect is to provide services for a fully designed building project irrespective of complexity or procurement method. It is also relevant where the architect is to provide other professional services. It is compliant with the requirements of the Housing Grants, Construction and Regeneration Act 1996, including reference to adjudication. Architects should not overlook the fact that this Act applies to construction consultancy services. To be at the receiving end of a referral to adjudication can be devastating, as a response is needed in a few days.

Article 5 gives the options of arbitration or legal proceedings. From the architect's point of view there are likely to be benefits in arbitration, for the following reasons:

- It is private, and the meetings or hearing can usually be arranged to suit the convenience of the parties, which is not usually the case in court.
- Third parties can be joined in only with the approval of the parties. This is likely to preclude the architect being sued jointly with the contractor or other consultants (unless brought into litigation as a third party).
- Clause 9.6 allows architects who are successful in arbitration to recover fees and expenses in respect of their own time, which may be considerable, whereas these are unlikely to be recoverable in litigation.
- If the suggestion of SFA/99 is followed the appointer of the arbitrator is likely to be the President of the RIBA, and an architect is likely to be appointed. This means the arbitrator is likely to understand the matters in dispute, but may set high standards for fellow professionals!

A note advises that:

> *Some amendments to the Conditions may be required where the Client is a Consumer and the Unfair Terms in Consumer Contracts Regulations 1994 apply or is a Residential Occupier under the Housing Grants etc Act 1996…*

The Unfair Contract Terms Act 1977 has the effect of rendering various exclusion clauses void, where they operate against 'a consumer' or where a party contracts on his or her own written standard terms of business. The Unfair Terms in Consumer Contracts Regulations 1994 apply to contracts with a consumer where the terms have not been individually negotiated. This would generally include standard forms such as SFA/99. An *unfair term* is any clause that causes a significant imbalance in the parties' rights to the detriment of the consumer. An indicative list of such terms is given in schedule 3 and includes

> *any term excluding or hindering the consumer's right to take legal action. … particularly by requiring the consumer to take the dispute to arbitration…*

It is important, therefore, that if the arbitration option is selected, or if any terms are proposed that could be seen as limiting the employer's rights, these have been explained and discussed (and the discussion minuted) so that they can be considered to have been individually negotiated.

SFA/99 includes provisions to comply with the HGR&CA in respect of Payment Notices, Interest on Late Payments, Suspension and Adjudication. That Act does not apply to work for a *residential occupier*. Nevertheless, its provisions may be incorporated into the architect's contract with a 'residential occupier', in which case they will apply.

On page 2 of SFA/99 there is an *Appendix to the Conditions* that includes the *Limit of Liability and Amount of Professional Indemnity Insurance Cover,* about which it is stated:

> Unless otherwise stated, PII cover, excluding legal costs, will be not less than the amount required by the Architects Registration Board.

ARB does not make reference to specific figures, but to *'adequate and appropriate'* cover.

The matter of PII was discussed in section 6.2 of Chapter 6.

Schedule 1 of SFA/99 is entitled *Project Description.* The *Notes for Architects on the Use and Completion of SFA/99* say that relevant matters may include:

- a brief description of the project
- site information – to be provided by the client
- other information – to be provided by the client
- construction cost:
  Identify the amount the Client wishes to spend on construction and, where possible, identify the budget for other elements i.e., fees, equipment/furniture, other costs.
  This point requires considerable caution. Many clients at the stage of appointing an architect will have unrealistic ideas about what their proposed building is going to cost. Acceptance by the architect of a low figure at this stage may subsequently come back to haunt the architect. There may be occasions when it will be inappropriate to enter a budget figure. No prudent architect guesses the construction cost: there is more chance of guessing it wrongly than correctly.
  The use of rates per square metre, so often unthinkingly bandied about, can turn out to be a landmine waiting to be trodden on a year or so hence. If reference has to be made to such rates it is better to use the fuller *BCIS Quarterly Review of Building Prices* than the abbreviated tables in standard cost books such as Spon's, but in every case it needs to be made clear that there are many factors that can cause deviation from a mean or mode rate, and that these rates do not usually include external works, allowance for inflation, VAT or fees. Strong written qualifications of any such rates are called for.
- time:
  Identify any key dates that the Client wishes to achieve.
  Similar comments are appropriate here as in respect of the budget. Acceptance by the architect of too tight a programme may end up with the client trying to sue the architect for failing to meet it. Again there may be some commissions where it will be inappropriate to include a timetable. No prudent architect guesses the construction programme. Guesses are more often wrong than right!

- third party agreements. Clause 7.5 reads:

Where the Client has notified, prior to the signing of this Agreement, that he will require the Architect to enter into an Agreement with a third party or third parties, the terms of which and the names or categories of other parties who will sign similar agreements are set out in an annex to this Agreement, then the Architect shall enter such agreement or agreements within a reasonable period of being requested to do so by the Client.

7.6 For the avoidance of doubt nothing in this Agreement shall confer or purport to confer on any third party any benefit or the right to enforce any term of this Agreement.

The foreword to *A Client's Guide to Engaging an Architect* makes this point:[2]

When it becomes part of our law, the Contracts (Rights of Third Parties) Bill will enable contracting parties to confer legally enforceable benefits upon others through their contracts. Developer clients may well use this provision to confer benefits upon purchasers, tenants and funders through their consultancy contracts. Architects will need to understand the facilitative provisions of the new law and be vigilant that Clients do not seek, through the appointments, to confer more benefits on third parties than the insurance community will give cover for. In the meantime, in order to prevent the unintentional conferring of such benefits the appointment excludes the operation of the Act, which is the prudent position to adopt.

Points to note here are:

- that the architect should not be entering into third party agreements unless the contractor and other consultants (and indeed the subcontractors undertaking design) are similarly bound
- that commercial clients are still likely to require warranties, at least until they get used to the working of this Act.

Schedule 2 of SFA/99 sets out the services to be provided by the architect. The first section is a bit confusing, as it appears that clauses 1 and 2 of Schedule 2 may be alternatives, which they are not. The definitions in the *Services Supplement: Design and Management* do not follow the Services 1–4 at the beginning of Schedule 2, where, in particular, there is no reference to Contract Administrator.

Schedule 2 includes a space for 'Other services'. These are listed on page 5 of SFA/99. They do not form part of 'the services' unless identified under 'Other services' on page 4. Any of these 'Other Services' that are to be included in the percentage or lump sum fee need to be spelled out and listed in Schedule 2, so that grounds for later misunderstandings are reduced to a minimum. It is made clear that otherwise these services 'will attract additional fees', and there is a section in Schedule 3 for 'Other fees'. They are divided, on page 5, into 'Activities' and 'Special activities'. The former are divided into three groups: 'Sites and buildings', 'Design skills' and 'Historic buildings and conservation'. Some of the more important headings under 'Activities' are as follows:

- *Selection of consultants.* This can involve additional work if the architect is asked to obtain competitive quotations from other consultants or to arrange and attend selection interviews for them.
- *Options appraisal.* It may be possible to meet a client's requirements in different ways. For example, additional space required by a client may be provided by a simple extension, or by the introduction of a mezzanine floor or by a new top floor; alternatively the client might move to a larger existing building, or to a new-build solution on a brown-field or green-field site. Consideration of the options will involve capital costs, timescale, disruption costs to the client's business caused by the works, and operational benefits of each option.
- *Compiling, revising and editing (a) strategic brief (b) detailed (written) brief and (c) room data sheets.* The normal architectural service does not include the preparation of the brief. However, there is inevitably a grey area between what may properly comprise the brief and what is initial design work. Many architects will see the preparation of room data sheets as part of the detailed design. It does not matter, provided both architect and client are aware what work the architect is going to do, and provided this is reflected in the fee arrangement.
- *Selection of sites and/or buildings.* Example: A specialist manufacturing company occupied a very constricted site near the centre of a small town. It wished to rebuild on a much bigger scale but, because of a specialist workforce in the area, did not wish to move far out of the town. Other relevant factors were the need for a substantial water supply, treatment and disposal of effluent, construction cost, environmental impact, access by public transport for operatives and access for large lorries. Three potential sites were identified, and the architect was asked to advise on the merits and drawbacks of each site.
- *Outline planning submissions.* A successful outline planning application may involve environmental impact and highway studies and prolonged negotiations with the planning authority. This work may well be outside the normal service.
- *Environmental studies.* The planning authority may ask for an environmental impact study.
- *Surveys, inspections or specialist investigations.* These might include measured surveys, topographical surveys, condition surveys of buildings that are to be altered or extended, structural investigations, ground investigations, CCTV surveys of existing drains or flues, tree surveys, or traffic surveys. Each such survey will need to be defined and have its limitations defined. It is particularly important that the architect does not take on responsibility for work

undertaken by others, and, where the architect is organising surveys and investigations by others, it must be made clear to both the employer and the surveyor that the contract is between them, with the architect acting only as agent for the employer in placing the specialist work. This is of immense importance in high-risk areas such as ground contamination, where the architect's PI cover may not extend to the work, and in such circumstances back-to-back contractual arrangements with the specialist company will be of no assistance to the architect if problems arise after that company has ceased to trade.

- *Accessibility audits*
- *Party wall matters.* Work under the Party Wall Act 1996 is referred to in section 9.12.3 below.
- *Two-stage tendering.* If two-stage tendering is to be adopted, the procedure should be agreed at the earliest opportunity and fees confirmed.
- *Negotiating a price with a contractor (in lieu of tendering).* Negotiated tenders are likely to give good overall value for most construction work, giving the benefit of a chosen contractor involved at a reasonably early stage, at a modest cost premium, which may be more than offset by a reduction in loss and expense and disruption claims, and with the probable advantage of quality work. Properly undertaken with the assistance of a quantity surveyor, a negotiated tender should not significantly increase architect's fees. Negotiated contracts may not be appropriate for public bodies.
- *Use of energy in new or existing buildings.* Increasing work is necessary to comply with those parts of the Building Regulations relating to energy conservation. This work is now required as a matter of course for almost all new buildings, and needs to be reflected in the basic percentage or lump sum fee. However, there are occasions when a client wants a building that is especially environmentally friendly or sustainable. In such cases it is likely that the design of the building and its services will involve research, development and detailed costing well above the norm. This needs to be reflected in the percentage fee, possibly by a reconsideration of the 'Class' into which the building falls.
- *Value management services.* Like project management, value management can mean what suits the person using the words. Amongst some prudent clients there is now an increasing emphasis on *costs in use and life cycle costing.* If different design solutions are going to be compared by reference to these criteria a lot of work will be involved, and this needs to be defined and priced for. Sadly much of British industry appears to be more interested in the bottom line of next year's balance sheet and the related executives' bonuses than in long-term planning.
- *Compiling maintenance and operational manuals.* The preparation of such manuals for the increasingly complex building services is outside the expertise of the average architect, and should be undertaken by the M & E consultant

or the relevant specialist subcontractors. However, the architect may be expected to prepare a maintenance manual for the building fabric and, if so, this should be specifically included and costed for. In practice the health and safety file under the CDM Regulations should go a long way towards the provision of a maintenance file. It may be that if the architect is also the planning supervisor (in which case there should be a separate formal appointment) there can be an add-on to that service to upgrade the health and safety file to a maintenance and operational manual.

- *Specially prepared drawings of a building as-built.* Again one would expect the as-built services drawings to be provided by the M & E consulting engineer or the services subcontractors, and for all the as-built drawings to be in the health and safety file. If the project has been built in accordance with the original drawings, the provision of as-built drawings should be easy. If there have been variations, the incorporation of these into the main drawings should have taken place and been paid for at the time.

- *Submission of plans for proposed works for approval of landlords, funders, freeholders, tenants etc.* In theory this should only be the cost of the prints of drawings, which will be covered by expenses. This clause should, however, protect the architect in the event of alterations having to be made to satisfy any of these parties. A typical case is the developer's shell building that requires modifications at a late stage to accommodate an incoming tenant's requirements.

- *Applications or negotiations for statutory and other grants.* There are many grant-giving trusts, but the one that architects are most likely to meet is the Heritage Lottery Fund. To prepare a good submission is a time-consuming task. Some applicants for such grants will be impecunious charities who will probably not be able to undertake their proposed project without Heritage Lottery funding, or grants from other sources such as *landfill tax.* Such clients may well put pressure on their architect to undertake work on the 'freebie basis' of *no grant – no fee.* Like all speculative work, this involves a tough commercial approach.

- *Interior design services*
- *Selection of furniture and fittings*
- *Design of furniture and fittings*
  What is meant by these three services? Most architects for most projects design such things as the wall, floor and ceiling finishes, fitted furnishings, colour scheme, light fittings, radiators, and blinds or curtains for major windows. Is the inclusion of 'Interior design services' in this list an indication of the architectural profession's further abdication of its role? Or does this refer to the design or choice of loose furnishings, crockery and cutlery? If the latter, the fee basis needs to be agreed. In some turnkey projects furnishings are included in the main building contract, and hence would be covered by a percentage fee.

- *Landscape design services.* Many architects have landscape design skills, particularly if a significant proportion of the landscaping is hard landscape. In many cases any such design work will be covered by the basic percentage fee.

- *Special drawings, photographs, models or technical information produced at the client's request.* These will normally be quoted for when the client requests them, often for a sales or fund-raising brochure.
- *Detailed inspection and report.* This is the first item under the heading 'Historic buildings and conservation', and is discussed under 'Surveys, inspections or specialist investigations' above.
- *Historical research and archaeological records.* What is to be done needs to be spelled out.
- *Listed building consents.* Listed building consent is required in addition to planning permission for work to listed buildings, although it would be usual to use the same drawings for both applications. This work would normally be covered by the basic percentage or lump sum fee, which would have been calculated taking the specialist building type into account.
- *Conservation area consents.* The position here is similar to that for listed building consents.
- *Grant-aided works.* What has been said above in respect of 'Applications or negotiations for statutory and other grants' is relevant here. However, in cases where a Heritage Grant is obtained for the repair of a listed building, there is likely to be a requirement to agree the specification with English Heritage and to make provision for EH's architect to inspect during the course of the works. This would normally be reflected in the basic percentage or lump sum fee for the type of building involved.
- *Exceptional negotiations with planning or other statutory authorities.* What is exceptional? In most planning applications an architect expects some discussions with the planners. Exceptional negotiations would include situations where public consultation was undertaken or, for example, where a traffic count was required.
- *Revision of documents to: (a) comply with requirements of planning or statutory authorities or landlord etc; (b) comply with changes in interpretation or enactment or revisions to laws or statutory regulations; (c) make corrections not arising from any failure of the architect.* In undertaking the design of a building, the architect has a responsibility to comply with statutory requirements. Thus (a) and (b) would apply only to cases where changes were required that could not reasonably have been foreseen by the architect. Section (c) covers the situation where the client, another consultant or a designing subcontractor has made mistakes in information provided. This clause might also apply to corrections necessitated by existing conditions, for instance ground conditions or archaeological remains that could not reasonably have been foreseen.
- *Ascertainment of contractor's claims.* These are likely to fall into the following categories:
  - *Extensions of time and the reasons therefor.* Given that the contractor may be

in delay as a result of his own or his subcontractors' faults, as well as a result of architect's instructions, exceptionally inclement weather etc., it is often difficult to establish causal links between potential causes of delay and actual delays. The situation is often very muddy. Tight competitive tendering encourages contractors to maximise delays that attract loss and expense payments and minimise those that do not. Under many contracts it will be the responsibility of the architect to assess the extensions of time and reasons therefor. However, notwithstanding the ultimate responsibility, on a complex project such assessment may well be outside the expertise of the architect, who may therefore need to take advice from a project planner using computerised programming. A problem is that such programming can often be manipulated to show any desired result. An added complication is that one of the matters attracting loss and expense payments is late information, and this could put the architect in the position of being both defendant and judge at the same time. Traditionally the architect sought initial advice from the quantity surveyor but, given the very tight fees for quantity surveying services, the latter is unlikely to wish to help. There will be occasions when the architect will need to advise the client to engage the services of a project planner, either directly, or as sub-consultant to the architect, to assist the architect in undertaking the contractual duties in respect of granting extensions of time.

— *Loss and expense claims arising out of delays and/or disruption of the progress of the works.* On a major project these claims can amount to millions of pounds. The architect will normally look to the quantity surveyor for initial advice, but huge amounts of work can be required from all the design team in assessing contractors' claims. They are a blight on the industry, fuelled by the naivety of those who still subscribe to the 'lowest contract sum = best value' syndrome. Any prudent architect who foresees a claim in the offing will do well to advise the client to engage a quantity surveyor or a claims consultant to prepare a draft response in advance of a possible referral to adjudication. Such a referral may have been carefully prepared over several months, before being dumped on the employer's desk with only perhaps seven days to respond to it.

It is a sad fact that a proportion of construction contracts do get into difficulties. At the first hint of this, intense management skills are needed to effect a rescue. Otherwise, and perhaps in any event, the contract will go from bad to worse, becoming confrontational and sour with everyone looking to whom they can attribute blame. Such contracts are highly stressful, and can be a nightmare for an architect. Nevertheless it needs to be said, and said repeatedly, loudly and clearly, that the majority of construction contracts of all types are completed on time, on cost, and free from material defect in design or construction.

• *Investigations and instructions relating to work not in accordance with the building contract.* The making of periodic inspections, particularly inspections prior to practical completion and at the end of the defects liability period, is part and parcel of the normal architectural service. However, this item covers the situation where, for example, a suspicion of a defect requires a trail to be followed, perhaps with extensive opening up, or a thermographic survey to ensure that insulation has been properly inserted into cavities, or a CCTV survey of the drains. If, for example, such a survey revealed backfall on a length of drain, there would need to be involvement by the architect into how the remedial works were to be dealt with and the extent to which the drain needed to be relaid. The situation would be more complicated if the drain ran under a building. As the remedial work would be undertaken at the contractor's expense, the architect would not get a percentage fee for any involvement, and there might be no contractual provision for fee recovery from the contractor in such circumstances. Any such involvement cannot of course be foreseen when the contract for architectural services is entered into, and this is therefore yet another clause to make it clear that such unforeseen and additional works are not covered by any percentage or lump sum fee.

- *Assessment of alternative designs, materials or products proposed by the contractor.* It is unlikely that this clause would apply to the checking of the contractor's design in a JCT Contract With Contractor's Designed Portion, as that would have been allowed for in the original fee agreement; nor would it apply to a case where the procurement method involved the appointment of the contractor at the pre-design stage and the contractor's proposals were made at that stage. It would apply to the situation where, during the course of the contract, the contractor wished to introduce an alternative method of construction or alternative materials because, for example, the originally proposed materials were found to be on extended delivery. In some such cases the matter might need investigation by the architect to the extent that it was not covered by the percentage or lump sum fee.

- *Dispute resolution services on behalf of the client, including any involvement with an adjudication between the client and another party.* Litigation, arbitration, adjudication, expert determination or mediation between the employer and the contractor, and possibly between the employer and another party, are likely to involve the architect in a huge amount of time. This is clearly outside the basic fee, and cannot be foreseen in advance. This clause is a safeguard in these circumstances.

- *Damage to or destruction of a building in construction or to existing buildings.* In the event of fire or storm damage the architect will be involved in a lot of extra work. The fees for this work are likely to be recoverable by the employer from insurers and/or the contractor. The architect's contract is with the employer, who is the first person to look to for payment of the additional fees.

- *Determination of any contract or agreement with any other party providing services to the project.* The determination of a contract is never undertaken lightly. The additional work for the architect flowing from the determination is likely to be considerable. Again, this is a situation that cannot be foreseen, and this clause spells out that it is not allowed for in the basic fee arrangement.

- *Insolvency of any other party providing services to the project.* Insolvencies create work, particularly the insolvency of a main contractor or major nominated subcontractor. This clause also applies to the insolvency of any of the consultant team. Again, such circumstances cannot be foreseen, and this clause safeguards the architect by excluding work under this head from the basic fee agreement.

- *Valuations for mortgage or other purposes.* In many cases funders release funds on architect's certificates, but occasionally some exceptional valuation may be required. Architects who are not qualified valuers should beware of giving 'open market valuations'.

- *Easements or other legal agreements.* These are the work of a solicitor, but the architect is likely to be asked to provide plans to attach to the deeds or agreements. The architect may also be asked to assist in determining boundaries, rights of light etc.

- *Investigation of building failures.* This may apply to a collapse during construction but is more likely to apply to defects that manifest themselves after practical completion, notably dampness, cracking, and ineffective or noisy air conditioning, heating or ventilation. This is a grey area, and the position is similar to 'Investigations and instructions relating to work not in accordance with the building contract', discussed above.

- *Feedback – post-completion evaluation.* This is another point that is a matter of degree. As part of the normal architectural service there will be at least one inspection at the end of the defects liability period, but in the unusual event of something significantly more being required, it will have to be paid for. A more likely scenario is that a client requiring an evaluation of the building and its procurement is likely to engage the services of someone entirely independent.

Thus, in summary, the lists of 'Other activities' in Schedule 2 provide a safeguard against subsequent misunderstandings of what was covered by the architect's fee and what was not.

Schedule 3 of SFA/99 is entitled 'Fees and expenses'. It commences with 'Work stage fees', which bears the note 'Identify Work Stages as in Schedule 2 and the clause number of the selected fee basis'.

The Work Stages are defined in the Conditions of Engagement, and follow the 1999 revised RIBA Work Stages, which are as follows:

- *A: Appraisal.* Identification of client's requirements and of possible constraints on development. Preparation of studies to enable the client to decide whether to proceed and to select the probable procurement method.
- *B: Strategic briefing.* Preparation of strategic brief by or on behalf of the client confirming key requirements and constraints. Identification of procedures, organisational structure and range of consultants and others to be engaged for the project.
- *C: Outline proposals.* Commence development of strategic brief into full project brief. Preparation of outline proposals and estimate of cost. Review of procurement route.
- *D: Detailed proposals.* Complete development of the project brief. Preparation of detailed proposals. Application for full development control approval.
- *E: Final proposals.* Preparation of final proposals for the project sufficient for coordination of all components and elements of the project.
- *F: Production information:*
  - F1: Preparation of production information in sufficient detail to enable a tender or tenders to be obtained. Application for statutory approvals.
  - F2: Preparation of further production information required under the building contract.
- *G: Tender documentation.* Preparation and collation of tender documentation in sufficient detail to enable a tender or tenders to be obtained for the construction of the project.
- *H: Tender action.* Identification and evaluation of potential contractors and/or specialists for the construction of the project. Obtaining and appraising tenders and submission of recommendations to the client.
- *J: Mobilisation.* Letting the building contract, appointing the contractor, issuing of production information to the contractor, and arranging site handover to the contractor.
- *K: Construction to practical completion.* Administration of the building contract up to and including practical completion. Provision to the contractor of further information as and when reasonably required.
- *L: After practical completion.* Administration of the building contract after practical completion. Making final inspections and settling the final account.

Four methods of establishing fees are referred to in the Conditions as follows:

- percentage fees
- lump sums
- time charges
- other agreed method.

Fees on these bases are discussed in Chapter 11.

Schedule 4 lists the 'Other appointments made under separate agreements by the client' and the 'Elements to be designed by others'. The importance of this page is set out in Clause 3.11:

> *The Client, in respect of any work or services in connection with the*
> *Project performed or to be performed by any person other than the Architect,*
> *shall:*
>
> *1. Hold such person responsible for the competence and performance of his services and for visits to the site in connection with the work undertaken by him*
>
> *2. Ensure that such person shall cooperate with the Architect and provide to the Architect drawings and information reasonably needed for the proper and timely performance of the services; and*
>
> *3. Ensure that such person shall, when requested by the Architect, consider and comment on work of the Architect in relation to their own work so that the Architect may consider making any necessary change to his work.*

These clauses are a safeguard for the architect when another party (other than a sub-consultant to the architect) does not perform. In particular they place a contractual obligation on the client to take responsibility for other parties who are to undertake work in connection with the project. This may include other consultants, the contractor, and subcontractors who provide design services. There may be difficulties in respect of the latter if they have not been listed in Schedule 4 and if warranties are not in place. With the above clause the architect will not be responsible for:

- delays by these other parties
- errors by these other parties.

Furthermore, if these parties cause delay or disruption to the architect he or she will be able to invoice the employer to cover the costs (and the employer should then be able to recover the sums from the defaulting party although this will depend on the terms of the employer's contract with that party).

The *Services Supplement: Design and Management* lists the architect's duties in some detail, in some cases with alternatives to be deleted and with provision for the inclusion of additional services. It is covered by a note:

> *This Supplement enables the Architect's design and management services, specific to a fully designed building project, to be tailored to suit the requirements of the Client on the Project.*

It is obviously important that the fee agreement be tailored to the needs of the particular client and project. The need for such tailoring of fee agreements is the primary raison d'être for this book.

The Conditions of Engagement set out the Work Stages and many other matters with which the architect needs to be familiar, including the following:

Communications 1.4

Communications, between the Client and the Architect. . . . .that are not in writing shall be of no effect unless and until confirmed in writing by the sender or the other party.

The architect who relies on a telephone call or a gentlemen's agreement is likely to be in difficulties.

Duty of Care 2.1

The Architect shall in performing the Services and discharging all the obligations under this Part 2 of these Conditions, exercise reasonable skill and care in conformity with the normal standards of the Architect's profession.

This is an important clause setting out the usually accepted standard for the services of a professional person. It is to be contrasted with fitness for purpose clauses, which impose a higher standard and may be applicable where one party is responsible for both design and construction. Such clauses are the standard for design and build contracts unless modified by specific contractual terms as, for example, in WCD98. Clients' solicitors instructed to draft bespoke terms of engagement for architects are likely to seek to introduce a 'fitness for purpose' clause, which should normally be met with outright rejection from an architect.

Appointment of Consultants or Other Persons 2.4

The Architect shall advise the Client on the appointment of Consultants or other persons, other than those named in Schedule 4, to design and/or carry out certain parts of the Works or to provide specialist advice if required in connection with the Project.

Appointment of Site Inspectors 2.5

The Architect shall advise the Client on the appointment of full-or part-time Site Inspectors, other than those named in Schedule 4, under separate agreements where the Architect considers that the execution of the Works warrants such appointment.

This is also discussed in Chapter 12, sections 12.4 and 12.9.

A prudent architect will never advise that site inspection is not necessary, but will bring to the client's attention the need to make a risk assessment in the light of the costs of a full-time or peripatetic clerks of works.

If the architect does not advise on the need for the involvement of others, the presumption may be that specialist designers or site inspectors are not considered to be necessary, and the inference could be drawn that the architect is undertaking any necessary specialist design work or site inspection.

An area of particular risk to the architect is the ever-more complex and expensive M & E works that are part of most modern buildings. If these are to be designed by a nominated or named specialist subcontractor the client needs to be so advised, and it needs to be clear who is going to check that the work has been done properly on site. The architect will not normally be qualified to do so, and the traditional clerk of works, usually from a background in joinery or bricklaying, will not have the expertise.

Visits to the Works 2.8

The Architect shall in providing the Services make such visits to the Works as the Architect at the date of the Appointment reasonably expected to be necessary.

This clause allows the architect to charge extra, on a time basis, if the number of site visits is increased beyond what was reasonably included for on appointment. Most architects will have had experiences where this has occurred, but the costs of additional visits are unlikely to be accepted unless somewhere there is clear evidence of what the architect did include for, and unless office records clearly record the number of visits made and the time involved: this highlights the need for a good time-recording system.

Appointment and Payment of Others 3.8

Where it is agreed Consultants, or other persons, are to be appointed, the Client shall appoint and pay them under separate agreements and shall confirm in writing to the Architect the services to be performed by such a person so appointed.

This needs to be read in conjunction with 2.4 and 2.5 above.

Site Inspectors 3.10 … shall be under the direction of the Lead Consultant…

This is a change in the traditional arrangement, whereby the clerk of works was usually under the direction of the architect.

Responsibilities of Others 3.11

The Client in respect of any work or service in connection with the Project performed or to be performed by any person other than the Architect, shall:

1. Hold such a person responsible for the competence and performance of his services and for visits to the site in connection with the work undertaken by him

2. Ensure that such a person shall cooperate with the Architect…

3.12

The Client shall hold the Principal Contractor and/or other contractors appointed to undertake construction works and not the Architect responsible for their management and operational methods, for the proper carrying out and completion of the Works in compliance with the building contract and for health and safety provisions on the site.

Traditionally a contractor has always been responsible for operations on site, and prudent architects endeavoured not to interfere. The underlying reason for 3.12 is the vexed area of what used to be called *supervision*. That term was in general use until about 20 years ago, and is still used in common parlance among solicitors and some older architects. However, supervision is now understood to mean the type of constant overlooking that is provided either by the contractor's foreman or site agent, or by the clerk of works or site inspector. Architects should not use the term in relation to their own services. *Architect's Appointment*, which preceded SFA/92, required the Architect to 'visit the site as appropriate to inspect generally the progress and quality of the work'. SFA/92 required the Architect, as part of the 'Basic services', to:

04 generally inspect materials delivered to the site.

05 as appropriate instruct sample taking and carrying out tests of materials, components, techniques and workmanship...

06 as appropriate instruct the opening up of completed work to determine that it is generally in accordance with the Contract Documents.

07 as appropriate visit the sites of the extraction and fabrication and assembly of materials and components to inspect such materials and workmanship before delivery to site.

08 at intervals appropriate to the stage of construction visit the Works to inspect the progress and quality of the Works and to determine that they are being executed generally in accordance with the Contract Documents.

It was generally understood that the architect needed to visit and inspect at critical points in the construction, but, subject to this, the architect would not be held liable for defective work that was likely to have been done and covered up between visits.

SFA/99 takes the matter further, and Section K of the *Services Supplement: Design and Management* includes the following:

1. Make Visits to the Works in connection with the Architect's Design.

This is very different, apparently relieving the architect of responsibility for site inspection, that is unless engaged as lead consultant and contract administrator. If, however, the architect is going to be named in a JCT form of contract, then this will entail having the inspection functions that are necessary to administer that contract, not least to enable the architect to issue the Certificate of Practical Completion and the Certificate of Making Good of Defects.

What all this is saying is that in an increasingly complex industry, with varied procurement methods, architects' post-contract functions are no longer standardised but must be thought through and defined in respect of each and every commission. Where they are not, there is a significant risk that architects will find themselves responsible for a great deal more than they intended.

Sub-Letting 4.2

The Architect shall not appoint any Sub-Consultants to perform any part of the services without the consent of the Client, which consent shall not be unreasonably withheld…

This matter is discussed further in Chapter 12, section 12.5.

Payment 5.11

The client may not withhold payment of any part of an account for a sum or sums due to the architect under the Agreement by reason of claims or alleged claims against the architect unless the amount to be withheld has been agreed by the architect as due to the client, or has been awarded in adjudication, arbitration or litigation in favour of the client and arises out of or under the Agreement. Save as aforesaid, all rights of set-off at common law or in equity which the client would otherwise be entitled to exercise are hereby expressly excluded.

This clause stops a client unilaterally making deductions from an architect's account in respect of claims against the architect, or setting off sums owed to, or claimed by, the client in respect of other projects. It does not of course stop a client withholding sums that are not due under the agreement.

Payment Notices 5.12

A written notice from the Client to the Architect:

2. Shall be given, not later than 5 days before the final date for payment of any amount due to the Architect if the Client intends to withhold payment of any part of that amount stating the amount proposed to be withheld and the ground for doing so or, if there is more than one ground, each ground and the amount attributable to it.

This clause follows the HGC&RA and means that if no notice has been given and an account remains unpaid after 30 days, it is likely to be recoverable within a couple of months using the adjudication process. The Act is also particularly important as it permits the architect to stop work if invoices are not paid. Given the very serious consequences that any such stoppage of work could have, this is not a strategy that any architect will employ lightly.

Payment on Suspension or Determination 5.16

Where the performance of the Services is suspended or determined by the Client, or suspended or determined by the Architect because of a breach of the Agreement by the Client, the Architect shall be entitled to payment of all expenses and other costs necessarily incurred as a result of any suspension ... or determination...

This puts an architect in a similar strong position to that of a contractor who suspends work or determines because of a breach by the employer.

Copyright

6.1 The Architect owns the copyright in the work produced by him in performing the Services...

One of the problems in connection with breach of copyright is that the damages may be very small. When entering into a commission an architect needs to assess the risk of the client using the architect's designs to obtain planning permission or to win a development opportunity and then ditching the architect. Where there is this risk the architect should seek to set out the payments required for the design work and for the subsequent use of the design if others are commissioned to take the project forward.

This can be a difficult area for an architect who undertakes design work 'at risk' for a developer. It is not good enough to merely state that fees will be chargeable if the scheme goes beyond a certain stage. It is necessary to agree the architect's terms of engagement in some detail before undertaking the 'at risk' work. The risk may be acute when there is a possibility that the developer, having obtained planning permission through the skill of the architect, decides to sell the site.

Limitation of Warranty by Architect 7.1

Subject always to the provisions of clause 2.1, the Architect does not warrant:

1. That the Services will be completed in accordance with the Timetable.

The architect cannot do so. Many factors may cause delays. However, this does not mean that the timetable can be ignored, because clause 2.1 requires the architect to use 'reasonable skill and care in conformity with the normal standards of the Architect's profession'.

Architect's Liability 7.3…

The Architect's liability for loss and damage… shall be limited to whichever is the lesser of the sum:

1. Stated in the Appendix; or

2. Such sum as is just and equitable for the Architect to pay having regard to the extent of his responsibility for the loss and/or damage in question when compared with the responsibilities of Contractors, Subcontractors, Consultants and other persons for that loss and/damage…

Traditionally all parties being sued were jointly and severally responsible for the entire loss. Thus an architect might expect to have been held responsible for 25% of a loss due to failures on inspection, but if the contractor was to go into liquidation, the architect would pick up 100%. This clause prevents such a situation.

Professional Indemnity Insurance 7.4

Professional indemnity insurance was discussed in Chapter 6, section 6.2.

8. Suspension and determination

This gives the architect the right to suspend services if the client is in default with payments of fees.

8.5 Determination

Determination is without prejudice to the accrued rights and remedies of either party.

9. Dispute Resolution

There is reference to adjudication in accordance with HGC&RA and, apart from certain small claims, there is provision for arbitration. Clause 9.6 allows the architect to recover the costs of time spent in arbitration or litigation with the former client, which would not otherwise be recoverable. From the architect's point of view there is probably an advantage in arbitration as opposed to litigation in that it prevents the scattergun approach of some lawyers, but it will not eliminate the possibility of the architect's being joined into litigation in court as a third party. In work for *consumers* arbitration may be excluded by the Unfair Terms in Consumer Contracts Regulations 1994.

9.2 Conditions of Engagement for Use with a Letter of Appointment (CE/99)

This is the second of the standard RIBA appointment documents. It replaces CE/95, which included a commendably simple *Memorandum of Agreement,* a *Schedule of Services* including 'other services for which additional fees are to be agreed', a *Schedule of Fees and Expenses,* and *Conditions of Appointment.* There was also a *Model Letter of Appointment from Architect to Client,* which emphasised some of the more important points. The intention was that the architect completed the document and the Memorandum was signed by both parties.

Its successor, CE/99, excludes the Memorandum of Appointment but includes the following to be completed:

- Schedule 1: Project description
- Schedule 2: Services
- Schedule 3: Fees and expenses
- Schedule 4: Other appointments
- Services supplement: Design and management
- Conditions of Engagement

The Conditions of Engagement are largely as SFA/99, but whereas in CE/95 the Memorandum of Agreement included clauses dealing with the time limit for making claims against the architect and the limitation of the amount of any such claims, CE/99 refers to these matters in the Conditions of Engagement, and requires time limits and the level of indemnity insurance to be specified in the letter of appointment and the appendix respectively. The latter appears to be a misprint, as there is no appendix, and the Model Letter of Appointment refers to both.

The intention with CE/99 is that the completed document together with a letter of appointment (the model for which is long and wordy) are sent to the client with the following instructions:

> *If these arrangements are acceptable to you, please sign the Agreement Clause below, initial the RIBA form where indicated in Schedule 1, the amendments (if any) to the Conditions (pages 8–12) and return all the documents to us. We will then countersign them and send you a certified copy set for your records.*

At the bottom of the letter there is an agreement to be signed by the two parties. The letter also indicates that the agreement does not take away statutory rights.

It seems that CE/95 and CE/99 were introduced because many architects, particularly in small and medium-sized practices (that is, most practices), were unhappy with SFA/92, which they saw as a seriously retrograde step from the previous document *Architect's Appointment*, which was well known, well understood, and could be sent to a client under cover of a very simply personalised letter. That document (the 'blue book') and its similar predecessor (the 'purple book') had served the profession well over a long period of time. The complaints about SFA/92 included the following:

- It was formal and complicated.
- Because it needed filling in throughout, clients were much more likely to want to negotiate terms, conditions and fees in their favour.
- Because it was obviously a legal document, some clients sent it to their solicitors, who responded with bespoke agreements in terms totally unacceptable. In one such case competent architects were to be commissioned to design a house extension including a swimming pool, and the bespoke agreement sent back following the submission of SFA92 included: 'The Architects hold themselves out as experienced in the design and supervision of swimming pools and warrant that the project will be fit for its purpose.' Negotiations proved in vain and the firm stepped down, leaving a less experienced practice who did not understand the significance of the wording to take its place.

While CE/99 perhaps has the advantage of a personalised letter to sign and return, CE/95 and CE/99 did not answer the criticisms of SFA/92, which can equally be applied to SFA/99. The sad truth probably is that the whole matter of appointing an architect has become so complicated that a simple system is impossible, but a number of architects consider that they would have been better served by something along the lines of *Architect's Appointment*.

The notes appended to CE/99 include the following:

Construction Cost

Identify the amount the Client wishes to spend on construction and, where possible, identify the budget for other elements i.e. fees, equipment/furniture, other costs.

Timetable

Identify any key dates that a Client wishes to achieve.

This information is to be provided by the client. Great caution is needed here. Experienced and competent architects will ensure that they qualify the recording of this information at this early stage, when information may be very sketchy. There are at least two reasons for this:

- Estimates before the brief is fully developed or at least some outline sketch proposals are prepared will probably be wrong, and the timescale will depend on many factors, not least the number of times the client has changes of mind during the design stages, the time taken by client committees or boards to approve proposals, and the lengthy time that is sometimes taken by planning authorities. Inevitably the first figure and time that are mentioned, however strongly these are qualified, will stick in the client's mind, and if, for any reason, they are exceeded the architect may be ill thought of.
- If subsequently, for whatever reason, the building costs more or takes longer than was initially indicated, the class of client that is always looking for a reason not to pay fees will find it here. When fees are sued for, a counterclaim is likely to follow, saying that the client was a total layman in all building matters and, having told his architect the budget and timetable, relied totally upon his architect to deliver.

9.3 Conditions of Appointment and a Schedule of Services for Use with a Letter of Appointment for Small Works (SW/99)

The headnote states:

SW/99 will be suitable for the provision of professional services:

- *Of a relatively straightforward nature where for instance the cost of construction works is not expected to exceed £150,000*
- *Where use of the JCT Agreement for Minor Works (MW98) might be appropriate*
- *Under a simple contract signed under hand*

SW/99 comes in a pad of 10 sets of two double-sided printed sheets, the first containing *Conditions of Appointment for Small Works* and the second *Schedule of*

Services for Small Works and *Other Activities.* In addition there is a *Model Letter of Appointment.* The letter sets out, inter alia, the basis of fees and times of payment. It makes reference to the enclosures, and at the bottom of the letter there is an agreement clause. A second copy of the letter is to be enclosed, and the client is asked to sign the agreement clause and return the copy letter to the architect.

The accompanying notes include the following:

> *A 'consumer' is a term applied to a Client who is 'acting for purposes which are outside his business' and the Unfair Terms in Consumer Contracts Regulations 1994 will apply. It is essential in such a case to explain the conditions and make whatever amendments are appropriate so that it can be agreed that terms have been individually negotiated in good faith. Note in particular that the conditions include an Arbitration clause but a consumer may opt for legal proceedings.*

> *The term 'residential occupier' under the Housing Grants, Construction and Regeneration Act 1996 means a party who 'occupies or intends to occupy (a dwelling) as his residence' to whom the statutory provisions in respect of Adjudication and payment regimes will not apply. Nevertheless the relevant conditions need not be removed from SW/99 if both parties so agree.*

SW/99 is a versatile document, and many architects may well consider it suitable for much larger contracts than those referred to in its head note. The conditions are a shortened version of SFA/99: they omit any reference to a limit of liability.

9.4 Amendment for Procurement of Employer's Requirements for a 'Design and Build' Contract: Amendment DB1/99

Where the procurement method is to be design and build, neither SFA/99 nor CE/99 is appropriate on its own. Amendment DB1/99, for use with either of these documents, is designed to meet these circumstances.

The extent to which the Employer's Requirements are taken will vary from job to job. In some cases it will be a performance specification; in others the project will be designed and specified in considerable detail, perhaps up to Work Stage F. The extent to which the Employer's Requirements are to be taken must be stated, as this will significantly affect the work and the fee level.

The following is the procedure for using the amendment DB1/99:

> *1. In SFA/99 at the end of Article 1 insert 'as modified by Amendment DB1/99 attached hereto' or, in the Letter of Appointment used with CE/99 refer to 'RIBA's*

Conditions of Engagement for the Appointment of an Architect (CE/99) as modified by Amendment DB1/99'.

2. Strike out any activities or Work Stages not required in the Services Supplement section of the Amendment.

3. Remove the Services Supplement (…from SFA/99 or strike out the Services Supplement in CE/99,… and attach the Amendment (pages DB1/99 A – C) to the inside cover of SFA/99 or CE/99.

If the procurement route is changed, after an initial appointment using SFA/99 or CE/99, from traditional procurement to design and build, then the agreement between client and architect should also be changed to reflect the very different responsibilities and liabilities of the architect. Where SFA/99 has been used the client and architect should either:

1. continue with the existing agreement but set down in a deed of variation, prepared with legal advice, the services completed and the new future services required by incorporating the DB1/99 Amendment, together with any consequential or other changes; or
2. agree to determine the performance of the architect's services under the existing SFA/99 agreement and enter into a new agreement incorporating DB1/99.

Where the Letter of Appointment has been used with CE/99 the client and architect may proceed with either of the options above, but the variation (option 1) would be incorporated into a carefully composed legal document, signed by both parties.

Where novation or consultant switch are contemplated the recommendation is that SFA/99 should be used with DB1/99 for the initial appointment of the architect to prepare the Employer's Requirements, which should include an additional recital 'foreshadowing a Tripartite Agreement between Client, Contractor and Architect'.

9.5 Contractor's Proposals Amendment where the Client is the Contractor under a 'Design and Build' Contract: Amendment DB2/99

This amendment is intended for use with SFA/99 where an architect is appointed by a contractor to prepare the contractor's proposals for a building project to be procured under the JCT Standard Form of Building Contract with Contractor's Design, or the JCT Form with Contractor's Designed Portion Supplement. The modifications to the conditions or to the services to be provided by the architect, as set out in this Amendment, can be tailored to suit the requirements of the specific contractor client and the project. These will largely depend on how far the Employer's Requirements have taken the design.

The use of DB2/99 is similar to that set out for DB1/99 above. However, it includes additional notes on consultant switch and novation, of which it states:

> The notes on Consultant Switch and Novation are intended purely as a starting point for discussion with legal advisors. The process of arranging a change in allegiance is complex whichever route is chosen. Architects would be unwise to attempt to draft the various documents themselves. Legal advice should always be obtained.

The notes in connection with the use of DB2/99 with consultant switch include:

> If the (Employer) Client, the Contractor and the Architect agree that the Architect is to prepare the Contractor's Proposals on behalf of the Contractor (Client) the procedure to be followed is briefly:

> 1. (Employer) Client, Contractor and Architect enter a Supplementary Agreement to permit the change in relationships and establish the rights of the three parties; and

> 2. Determination of performance of the Services by the Architect under his Agreement with the (Employer) Client; and

> 3. the Architect and Contractor enter Amendment DBS/99 with SFA/99…

> NB: The Initial Agreement between Architect and Client should use SFA/99, Amendment DB1/99 and include an additional article foreshadowing the Supplementary Agreement.

With reference to the use of DB2/99 with novation, the notes state:

> If the (Employer) Client, the Contractor and the Architect agree that the Architect's Agreement is to be novated to the Contractor for the preparation of the Contractor's Proposals the procedure to be followed is briefly:

> 1. A (Deed) of Variation is drawn up by the parties to vary the Agreement with the original Client (SFA/99 and DB1/99) to incorporate any necessary amendments to the Schedules in SFA/99 and pages C–E of Amendment DB2 (The Articles, Appendix and Attestation in DB2 are discarded)

> 2. Employer, Contractor and Architect enter a Novation Agreement and the Contractor replaces the Employer as Client.

The wording of the above is an indication of just how difficult and complex the issues of consultant switch and novation are. They are discussed in Chapter 14, sections 14.3 and 14.4, and are best avoided.

An area of difficulty in working for the contractor is that initial work may be done 'at risk' and in a very short time. Subsequently, when the contractor's price has been accepted, it may be found that the contractor is responsible for work that has not been priced.

Example
In the conversion of an existing building under a design and build contract, a serious defect in the building came to light as soon as work started on site. Because of a catch-all amendment to the JCT standard form, the contractor could not recover the costs of the rectification work and sought to recover the costs incurred from the architect.

If the contractor is pricing on sketch drawings the architect must ensure he or she is adequately protected. If an existing building is involved the architect should ask for a building survey report, or, if intending to actually do the survey, make sure the terms of engagement include suitable qualifications, as referred to in section 9.12.2 below.

9.6   Employer's Agent

There is no standard form for the engagement of an Employer's Agent under WCD98, but it is covered by SFA/99 with DBI/99, which, as quoted and discussed in Chapter 7, section 7.2.1, can be used, with appropriate descriptions of the services to be provided.

Article 3 of WCD98 states:

AB or such other person as the Employer shall nominate in his place for the purpose shall be the Employer's Agent referred to in clauses 5.4 and 11 and, save to the extent which the Employer may otherwise specify by written notice to the Contractor, for the receiving or issuing of such applications, consents, instructions, notices, requests or statements or for otherwise acting for the Employer under any other of the Conditions.

Basically this is a contract administration role, but there is a potential hazard arising from the Third Recital:

…the Employer has examined the Contractor's Proposals and the Contract Sum Analysis and… is satisfied that they appear to meet the Employer's Requirements.

Is it the role of the Employer's Agent to examine the contractor's proposals? If so, to what extent? Merely from the point of view of spatial requirements, or should this compliance check extend far beyond that, to technical details, and even to the extent of calculations? This needs to be specified in the agent's terms of engagement, bearing in mind that DB1/99 includes:

> Coordinating review of recommended Contractor's Proposals

There is further discussion of the checking of drawings in section 9.12.5 below.

9.7 Form of Appointment as Sub-Consultant (SC/99)

This agreement is intended for use:

- when a consultant is required by the client to provide an all-in consulting service and thus has to engage sub-consultants
- when a consultant chooses to engage sub-consultants: in this case the client's approval should normally be obtained to comply with section 1.5 of the *RIBA Code of Professional Conduct.*

The important point to note, and it is stressed in the headnote of this agreement, is that the consultant will retain the primary liability to the client regardless of the nature of the sublet work. This means that the consultant must ensure:

- that the sub-consultant's PI insurance covers the work to the full extent of the consultant's limit of liability, and has no relevant onerous exclusions
- that the consultant's own PI insurance will cover any claims that cannot be passed down the line to the sub-consultant because the sub-consultant has ceased trading or for some other reason no longer has insurance cover
- that the sub-consultant's contractual liability will equate to that of the consultant: that is, if the main consultancy contract is by deed, the sub-consultancy must also be by deed.

SC/99 contains conditions derived from SFA/99. It includes a useful note by Mark Klimt, solicitor, previously published in the *RIBA Journal* in July 1998, and a draft Warranty Agreement (SC/99[W]) between the sub-consultant, client and consultant. This is a complex affair, and if such documentation is required advice should be sought from an experienced construction lawyer.

There is further discussion about sub-consultants in Chapter 12, section 12.5.

9.8 Form of Appointment as Project Manager for a Construction Project (PM/99)

The headnote commences:

> *PM/99 is suitable for a wide range of projects where the Client wishes to appoint a Project Manager to provide a management service and/or other professional services.*

This document follows SFA/99 quite closely, and covers little more than what is normally provided by any lead consultant (and was traditionally provided by the architect as a matter of course), although there is scope for the document to be expanded to cover anything.

It is fashionable to have a project manager, whatever the term means – see Chapter 12, section 12.3. As with most of these appointments, the important thing is to specify exactly what is going to be done and what fees are to be paid for doing it.

9.9 Form of Appointment as Planning Supervisor (PS/99)

This form may be used for the appointment of any suitably qualified construction professional as planning supervisor under the CDM Regulations 1994. Architects need to take care to ensure their clients do not expect them to provide 'planning supervision' services within the fee for basic architectural services. Planning supervision is further referred to in section 9.12.4.

9.10 Historic buildings

Both SFA/99 and CE/99 are suitable for use in connection with the repair or conservation of historic buildings. SFA/99 and CE/99 list under the heading 'Other activities' a number of exclusions from the normal services for a building project, but with provision for these to be included in the appointment from the outset by identifying them in Schedule 2: Services as 'Other services'. In the case of historic building projects, the document *A Guide to RIBA Forms of Appointment 1999 and other Architect's Appointments* lists the 'special services' that may be required for commissions involving alterations and repairs to, and conservation of, historic buildings. These services are listed under the following headings:

- *HB1 Detailed Inspection and Report.* This covers advice on the need for and extent of opening-up of the fabric, archival research, detailed inspections, feasibility of alterations, recommendations for repair in order of priority, measured surveys, integrating the work of other consultants or conservators, and reporting.

- *HB2 Historical Research and Archaeological Records.* This covers the carrying out and coordination of historical research, investigative analyses, and the recording of details as opening-up takes place.
- *HB3 Statutory Consents (Work Stage D).* This refers to making applications for Listed Building Consent and/or Conservation Area Consent.
- *HB4 Grants.* This does not specifically refer to making grant applications, but by implication it is included. It does refer to the providing of information and completion of forms supporting claims for payment of grants.

9.11 Community architecture

The publication *A Guide to RIBA Forms of Appointment 1999* contains a *Supplementary Schedule for a Community Architecture Project* to be used in conjunction with SFA/99 or CE/99.

Community architecture (CA) services relate to commissions where the intended end-users are involved in the design process, notwithstanding the fact that they are not the paying client.

Example
A housing association came to an arrangement with a cooperative whereby the association would finance a scheme incorporating housing and space for small-scale cooperative businesses. On completion the cooperative was to purchase the development with the aid of a mortgage from a bank. Some of the cooperative enterprises were to assist in the construction of the project and its subsequent maintenance. Unfortunately the lines of communication were blurred. Relationships between the cooperative and the housing association deteriorated. The costs of the project escalated, and the cooperative was unable or unwilling to obtain the intended mortgage, leaving the housing association holding the baby.

Another potential client body in this field is a group of self-build householders. Such schemes are fraught with difficulties.

Example
A firm of consultants held itself out as advisers to self-build housing associations. It assisted with the formation of the association and the raising of money by way of a bank loan, to be repaid by mortgages on the individual houses when they were complete. The firm purported to design and manage the construction

project, and for this work took a very significant fee. Long before the houses were complete the bank loan was all spent, leaving the self-builders unable to finish their properties. It then came to light that the consultants had found a valuer who had overvalued the land, and the consultants had grossly underestimated the construction costs. By this time the firm of consultants, a limited liability company, had taken its substantial fees and was no longer trading, leaving the bank, the sub-consultants and the self-builders in great difficulties.

In CA projects it is vital to distinguish between the paying client, as defined in SFA/99 or CE/99, and the secondary end-user client, who may play a critical role throughout the design and construction but with whom there may be no contractual nexus. To assist in the clarification of this distinction there are additional conditions of appointment for CA projects where the end-user is not the contractual client. These are intended to overcome any problems in connection with lines of communication or authority.

Systematic administrative procedures are vital for CA projects. Additions or amendments to the architectural services need to be confirmed promptly and accurately to all parties. Because of the difficulties of assessing in advance the time that will be taken with this sort of work, it is most appropriately charged for on a time basis. If this is not acceptable to the client, a compromise may be that certain specified services are on the basis of an agreed lump sum, with other services on a time basis.

Example

A social housing scheme developed serious defects after the Final Certificate had been issued. Another architect was commissioned to investigate and make recommendations. The remedial works required some tenants to be decanted. There was obvious concern about tenant claims. A site-based architect was engaged to liaise with the remedial works contractor and to act as both clerk of works and tenant liaison officer. While not strictly 'community architecture', the fairest way to both parties for charging for this work was on a time and expenses basis at agreed rates.

9.12 Other services

SFA/99 contains in Schedule 2 a list of 'Other activities', many of which were listed in section 9.1. There is no end to the additional services that an architect can provide. The same advice applies to these as to normal architectural services, namely:

- that the services are defined
- that the fees payable are defined

- that the architect has the expertise and resources
- that the work is covered by the architect's PII.

Some of many other services are mentioned below.

9.12.1 Dispute resolution

There are several possible roles in which the architect might be involved here, including:

- expert witness
- joint expert
- expert determinator
- conciliator
- mediator
- adjudicator
- technical assessor
- arbitrator.

An architect should not be undertaking work in any of these fields without some specialist knowledge and, in some cases, extensive training and further qualifications. Important points to take into account include the following:

- Who is the client? When a solicitor instructs an expert, the solicitor will be responsible for the expert's fees, unless the letter of instruction spells out that the solicitor is instructing as agent for the client who will be responsible for the expert's fees.
- When acting in a role that is providing a decision or award (which one or even both of the parties may not like) the architect should try to ensure that there is a provision for payment prior to their taking up the decision or award. This may be difficult with adjudications under JCT contracts as the JCT scheme does not allow for it, but it is nevertheless usually done.
- When instructed as joint expert the architect should seek agreement as to which solicitor is to be responsible for payment of his fees. If the solicitors seek to shuffle the responsibility directly to the parties the joint expert may need to ask for money up front to be held in the client's account.
- If instructed as expert determinator or joint expert the architect should seek to include an indemnity clause, similar to that included by statute for adjudicators and arbitrators. This is desirable because one party will probably not like the decision and, if there is considerable money at stake, is likely to challenge it.
- When acting as expert witness the architect needs to be aware of Chapter 35

of the Civil Procedure Rules, which require the expert to 'assist the Court' and to include appropriate declarations.

- There is a specimen form for the appointment of a conciliator at the back of *A Guide to RIBA Forms of Appointment 1999*. The JCT publishes a form for the appointment of an adjudicator. The Academy of Experts publishes *Model Terms of Engagements for an Expert*. Most arbitrators have their own terms of engagement.
- In cases where time has to be set aside for hearings, the architect should consider including some form of cancellation charge in the event of the matter settling. This is done as a matter of course by most arbitrators, but is more difficult for experts. Having to set aside blocks of time for hearings can be very disruptive to diary management, especially as 95% of cases settle before trial.

Initiation into this field of work for most architects will be an appointment to act as an expert witness. Before doing so, an architect should read not only CPR 35, referred to above, but also the judgement of HHJ Richard Seymour QC in The Royal Brompton Hospital NHS Trust case against its consultant team. This area of work offers opportunities for architects who have the ability to think logically and clearly. Professor John Uff QC writes:

> Curiously, at the Centre of Construction Law at King's College, architects have always represented the smallest number of applicants within the construction industry professions, although it should also be emphasised that those who have taken up construction law in this way have often achieved distinguished results. As a member of the Bar I have always found it most difficult to find an adequate number of experienced architects to act as expert witnesses or arbitrators, in contrast to the sister professions of quantity surveying and engineering.[3]

Perhaps this may change?

9.12.2 Surveys

The important point to note is that any limitations must be set out when the contract to undertake the survey is entered into. Limitations cannot normally be introduced later on. A particularly important point is to know why the survey is required. This will largely determine what has to be done.

There are differing approaches to defining the extent of a survey. Some prefer a positive approach defining what will be done; others prefer an approach that lists what will not be done. The following is a simple list of exclusions to include in a contract for a building survey of a residential property. In the case of a flat it will normally be necessary to inspect the entire building, as each flat owner is likely to be responsible for a proportion of the costs of maintaining the main structure, external works and main services.

- The woodwork or other parts of the building that are covered, unexposed or inaccessible to the surveyor without the assistance of a carpenter or other person, or without a ladder in excess of 3 m, will not be inspected. Where the property is furnished at the time of the survey those parts of the building covered by furniture and/or floor coverings will not be fully inspected. It will not therefore be possible to report conclusively that these parts of the property are free from defect.
- Trial holes to determine subsoil conditions or foundation sizes, and theoretical calculations to check sizes of structural elements, will not be made, nor will tests to determine the presence or otherwise of high alumina cement. Laboratory tests on mortar, plasterwork, etc. will not be made.
- Tests of service installations or drains involving the attendance of specialist consultants and/or the use of special equipment will not be carried out. Flues will not be tested.
- Full investigation of title, tenure, covenants, rights of way, planning approvals, clearance orders, improvement lines, NHBC certificates, etc., normally involving the services of a solicitor, will not be carried out.
- Where building or repair costs are given, they are for guidance purposes only and should not be construed as quotations or estimates. They should be substantiated (prior to exchange of contracts) by proper competitive quotations or estimates from appropriate contractors.

With commercial buildings, similar limitations are necessary. Where the property is leased, a copy of the lease must be seen to establish the repairing obligations, which can be very onerous. Where part of a building is being leased, it will be necessary to inspect the whole of the main structure, common parts, services etc., as each tenant is likely to be responsible for a proportion of the costs of repair and maintenance of these elements. In all commercial buildings it is likely to be necessary for an M & E consultant to be engaged to inspect the services, either as a direct appointment of the client or as a sub-consultant.

Inspections of buildings under construction can be onerous, and once again the extent of the inspections must be clearly defined, together with the limitations. Work that is covered up between visits cannot be inspected, but the presumption may be otherwise if this is not stated. Similarly it is necessary to state the frequency of visits. If visits are to be made at specific key times, such as before constructing the foundations or before backfilling drains, arrangements for reasonable notice to the architect need to be written into the contract.

9.12.3 Party walls

The Party Wall etc. Act 1996 extended, in a slightly modified form, the provisions that for decades had applied in London (by reason of the London Building Acts) to the rest of the country. In summary the Act requires that where work is to take place that affects a party wall (as defined in the Act) or a party boundary structure, or work is to foundations within 3 m or in some cases 6 m of an adjoining owner's building, the building owner is required to serve notice on the adjoining owner, of either one month or two months depending on the type of work. The two parties may then appoint an agreed surveyor or, more usually, each party appoints its own surveyor and in the event that they are unable to agree they appoint a third surveyor. Where this Act is going to apply, it is important that the architect flags it up to the client at an early stage, not least because otherwise it may lead to delays and at worst an injunction by the adjoining owner stopping the work and possibly leading to expensive contractual claims.

In many cases the work of the party wall surveyor is relatively simple, but in other cases, particularly where there are many ownerships involved, multistorey buildings, proposed new deep basements, or adjoining owners who are difficult to trace or are determined not to cooperate, considerable skill and experience is necessary. Many architects will feel confident to undertake simple party wall cases, but in more complex cases the work will be limited to those architects who have undertaken training in this area or are qualified by experience. Party wall work may be a useful additional source of income for an architectural practice if there is someone who specialises in the field.

Because the party wall surveyor has statutory duties, this appointment should be entirely separate from the appointment of the architect. The normal arrangement will be on an hourly rate basis. The adjoining owner's surveyor will need to enter into a contract with his or her client, normally by exchange of letter, but will seek to ensure that the party wall agreement includes a clause that the building owner will reimburse the adjoining owner for fees paid to the latter's surveyor. A third surveyor will require a simple form of appointment signed by or on behalf of both parties on a joint and several basis.

9.12.4 Planning supervision

The Construction (Design and Management) Regulations 1994 introduced the terms *planning supervisor* and *principal contractor* to the industry, both confusing terms in that they relate entirely to health and safety matters.

The CDM Regulations apply generally to construction work that is notifiable: that is, work that lasts for more than 30 days or will involve more than 500 person-days of work. CDM also applies to non-notifiable work that involves five people or more on site at any one time. However, CDM applies to any design work no matter how briefly the work lasts or how few workers are involved on site. If the work includes demolition, CDM applies regardless of the length of time or the number of workers. Work for a domestic owner-occupier is excluded, except for the requirements on designers and for the project to be notified to the HSE.

Any architect should be able to undertake the work of a planning supervisor subject to appropriate training or experience, and this work may provide useful additional income for an architectural practice that has a member who chooses to specialise in it. Because this is an appointment under statutory regulations, it is appropriate that it is separate from the appointment as architect.

The RIBA publishes a *Form of Appointment as Planning Supervisor* (PS/99), which contains similar conditions of engagement to SFA/99. Schedule 2. The section on the Planning Supervisor's Services commences:

> *The Planning Supervisor shall:*
>
> *1. Perform the Services necessary for completion of the Work Stages indicated below and in the table 'Normal Services'.*
>
> *2. Prepare the pre-tender Health and Safety Plan and the Health and Safety File for the Project.*
>
> *3. Perform any other activities identified below.*
>
> *4. Perform any other Services identified below.*

It then goes on to list seven 'Other activities' under the headnote:

> *These activities do not form part of the Services unless the reference number is circled. Performance of any of these activities will attract additional fees in accordance with Clause 5.6.*

These include:

> *OA.01 advise Client on prospective Designers additional to Service 1.11 in relation to CDM Regulations and their health and safety policies and procedures, and attend interviews as necessary.*

Service 1.11 limits advising the client on 'a maximum of 6 prospective designers'.

> OA.02 advise Client on prospective tenderers additional to Service G.2 in relation to the CDM Regulations, and attend interviews as necessary.

G2 limits advising the client to 'a maximum of 6 prospective tenderers'.

OA.04 covers design variations, and OA.07 covers the correction of defects if this is notifiable as a separate project under the Regulations.

Clause 5 gives the option for payment of fees on a percentage basis, lump sum basis or time charge. There is a somewhat unusual provision for a 'licence fee under Clause 6.2' to enable the client

> to copy and use… drawings, documents and bespoke software produced by the Planning Supervisor in performing the Services… for purposes related to the Project on the Site or part of the Site to which the design relates.

Planning supervision may look easy work, but the risk is of a serious incident on site. When this occurs, the planning supervisor may be in difficulties if the supervision work has not been done properly. In the year to April 2001, 106 workers and eight members of the public were killed in construction accidents. The police and HSE now respond, often within hours, to work-related fatalities and serious injuries with a view to bringing manslaughter charges against individuals and companies where appropriate. Corporate manslaughter charges are now being brought at a rate of more than one a month. This is not a time for planning supervisors to take risks: they may need to be tough, and decree that work cannot commence until adequate health and safety documentation is in place.

9.12.5 Checking of drawings

An architect may be engaged to check drawings under a design and build or PFI contract, or for compliance with Building Regulations. This can be high-risk work. Thus it is essential to check that those who have prepared the drawings are engaged under proper contracts and have adequate PI insurance.

The extent of the checking must be defined. For example, does it extend to:

- specialist subcontractor's drawings?
- coordination?
- calculations?
- dimensioning?

A problem may be that the drawings provided are correct in what they show, but have omissions.

9.12.6 Development monitoring

The architect may be engaged by the prospective tenant (who will have full repairing obligations) or a funder, to provide development monitoring services. This is likely to involve checking that contractual documentation and insurances are in order, checking drawings and possibly calculations and monitoring work on site by way of periodic visits.

The service and limitations need to be clearly specified.

9.12.7 Facilities management

Facilities management is a current buzz description for what has always been done by the traditional works engineer, estates bursar or property manager. It can cover a vast area of work, including management, lettings, maintenance, alterations, caretaking and cleaning, health and safety, security, insurances, communications, IT, estate records, furnishings and possibly staff catering and transport.

The British Institute of Facilities Management defines it thus:

> *Facilities Management is the instigation of multi-disciplinary activities within the built environment and the management of their impact upon people and the workplace.*

There is no reason why architects cannot undertake this work, buying in the skills they do not have in house.

Again, exactly what is to be done and how and when it is to be paid for must be clearly set out.

9.13 Bespoke agreements

It is open to the parties in any contract to agree their own bespoke terms and conditions, but an architect whose client's solicitor draws such terms and conditions will be wise to have them vetted by his or her own legal advisor, not least because such agreements often seek to transfer all risks to consultants and sometimes include requirements that are uninsurable.

In large, complex multi-party projects, bespoke agreements are essential.

9.14 Standard forms of building contract

This section flags up a warning. Most standard forms of building contract require the insertion of the name of the 'architect' or 'contract administrator' (or 'engineer' or 'project manager'). Any architect or other consultant who allows his or her name to be inserted into a standard form of building contract is, by implication, indicating that he or she will be carrying out the functions required of the architect or other consultant under that standard form. This is likely to involve:

- provision of production information at the right time
- issuing of architect's instructions
- issuing of certificates of non-completion
- making grants of extensions of time
- issuing of interim certificates for payment (and if also named as quantity surveyor, or if no quantity surveyor is named, probably making, or at least checking, interim valuations)
- making periodic inspections, especially at crucial stages and before issuing certificates for payment, and at practical completion
- making post-practical completion inspections and issuing a certificate of making good of defects
- issuing the final certificate.

These functions will need to be undertaken, whether or not they are covered by the architect's contract of appointment, if the architect has agreed to be named in the contract. It is vitally important that all the project documentation is consistent.

Example
An architectural technician was commissioned to prepare working drawings for a scheme. Subsequently the client's funding bank required a JCT form of contract to be used. The technician's name was entered as contract administrator. He was aware of this. Neither he nor his client understood the contract, and the technician did nothing further as he believed he had been commissioned only to prepare drawings. There were claims from the builder. The technician was in difficulties because he had allowed his name to be entered into the standard form of contract. There was an implication that he had undertaken to carry out the contract administrator's duties.

If the architect inserts his or her name (or allows it to be inserted) as quantity surveyor in a standard form, the implication is that this entails the provision of quantity surveying services, whether or not there is extra payment for them.

Example

An architect's client did not want to pay for a quantity surveyor. The architect agreed to certify on the basis of contractor's valuations. The architect inserted his name as quantity surveyor in the standard JCT Form of Contract. He failed to appreciate that a valuation was seriously front-loaded. The contractor went into liquidation part way through the project. The architect faced adjudication for over-certification.

Further reading

J. Anstey *Party Walls and What to Do with Them* 5th edn (RICS Books, 1998).

*ARB *Code of Professional Conduct and Practice* (Architects' Registration Board, 1997).

BCIS *Quarterly Review of Building Prices* (RCIS/BCIS).

C. Bond, M. Solon and P. Harper (ed. S. Burn) *The Expert Witness in Court: A Practical Guide* 2nd edn (Shaw, 1999).

D. Chappell *Understanding JCT Standard Building Contracts* 6th edn (E & FN Spon, 2000).

S. Cox and A. Hamilton *Guidance for Clients on Party Wall Procedures: The Party Wall etc Act 1996* (RIBA Publications, 1997).

C.C. Delemore *Copyright Explained* (RIBA Publications, 1994).

P. Hibberd and P. Newman *ADR and Adjudication in Construction Disputes* (Blackwell Science, 1999).

M. Hollis and C. Gibson *Surveying Buildings* 4th edn (RICS Books, 2000).

HSE *CDM Regulations: How the Regulations Affect You* (free leaflet suitable to give to clients).

O. Luder *A Guide to Keeping Out of Trouble* rev. and extended edn, Chapters 1 and 2 (RIBA Publications, 2001).

*D. Mosey *Design and Build in Action* (Chandos, 1998).

J.R. Murdoch and P. Murrells *Law of Surveys and Valuations* (Estates Gazette, 1995).

M.P. Reynolds *The Expert Witness in Construction Disputes* (Blackwell Science, 2001).

Code of Professional Conduct and Standard of Professional Performance (RIBA Publications, 1997).

Architect's Appointment: Historic Buildings – Repairs and Conservation Work (RIBA Publications, 1990).

Architect's Guide to Job Administration: The Party Wall etc Act 1996 (RIBA Publications, 1997).

*A *Client's Guide to Engaging an Architect (Including Guidance on Fees)* rev. edn (RIBA Publications, 2000).

*A *Client's Guide to Engaging an Architect: Small Works Only* rev. edn (RIBA Publications, 2000).

*R. Phillips (ed. S. Lupton and M. Lane) *The Architect's Contract: A Guide to RIBA Forms of Appointment 1999 and other Architect's Appointments* (RIBA Publications, 1999).

Engaging an Architect: Guidance for Clients on Health and Safety: The CDM Regulations 1994 rev. edn (RIBA Publications, 1996).

Engaging an Architect: Guidance for Clients on Party Wall Procedures: The Party Wall etc. Act 1996 rev. edn (RIBA Publications, 2001).

A. Spedding (ed.) *CIOB Handbook of Facilities Management* (Longman, 1994).

S. Summerhayes *CDM Regulations Procedures Manual* (Blackwell Science, 1999).

Notes

1 A. Blackler, Foreword in *A Client's Guide to Engaging an Architect (Including Guidance on Fees)* rev edn (RIBA Publications, 2000).

2 Ibid.

3 J. Uff *Are We All in the Wrong Job? Reflections on Construction Dispute Resolution,* p 4 (Society of Construction Law, 2001).

10   The pre-SFA agreement

When first engaged to undertake a commission it may not be possible to enter into a formal SFA/99 or similar agreement, although there may be much to be gained by doing so at this first instance and subsequently amending if necessary. The *RIBA Code of Professional Practice* states at 3.2 that to uphold Principle Three a member undertakes:

> When offering services as an independent consultant, not to quote a fee without receiving an invitation to do so and sufficient information on the nature and scope of the project to enable a quotation to be prepared which clearly indicates the services covered by the fee.

Reasons why it may not be practical to enter into a full SFA/99 or similar agreement might include the following:

- The client may not know what they want or need, and may require assistance with the preparation of a brief. The architect should note that SFA/99 includes the revised RIBA Work Stages, and that Stages A and B, which were previously headed 'Inception' and 'Feasibility' and were excluded from the basic percentage fee, are now headed 'Appraisal' and 'Strategic briefing' and included in the basic fee. See section 9.1 in Chapter 9.
- The site may not be agreed, and the client may require assistance with the choice of site or an existing building to be purchased. This work should normally be undertaken on a time basis.
- Because the above information is not to hand, the cost of the project may not be known – nor indeed whether or not it will be new-build or work to an existing building. If this is the case the architect will not be in a position to agree fees. However, there is nothing to stop an agreement being entered into on the basis of the RIBA indicative percentage fee scales published in *A Client's Guide to Engaging an Architect (Including Guidance on Fees)*.
- The procurement method may not be known. However, this does not preclude going forward with SFA/99 and then introducing one of the amendments DB1/99 'Employer's requirements' or DB2/99 'Contractor's proposals' if design and build is the subsequently chosen procurement route.
- It may not be known whether the architect is also to be design leader and/or lead consultant and/or contract administrator and/or project manager and/or construction manager. This may be a more difficult area, but assumptions might be made on the best information available, dealing with any subsequent alterations by way of an addendum to the agreement or an exchange of letters.
- Is the architect to undertake the role of planning supervisor? This is something

that is discrete and is probably best left over for an entirely separate agreement using PS/99.

- The client may not wish to make a commitment to a formal agreement at this early stage, in which case a letter is called for setting out the preliminary work that it is agreed will be done and the terms of engagement for it. A duplicate of the letter might be enclosed with the request that the client sign an endorsement, along the following lines:

I/We confirm that the Preliminary Services are to proceed in accordance with the terms and conditions set out above.

However, not all clients will return such a letter, and an architect may not wish to rock the boat at this initial stage. The important thing is to agree what is to be done and to confirm it in writing. It is all too easy for an architect to be so excited with a new project that he or she crashes ahead with nothing confirmed. Here is a salutary reminder to have at least an initial fee agreement in place from day 1:

Example

A practice was invited to act for a consortium in making a bid for a development. It was a two-stage competition. The architect agreed to do Stage 1 at risk but, if successful in getting to Stage 2, was to be paid for the Stage 2 work whether successful in that stage or not. The understanding was that the architect, if successful in Stage 2, would be commissioned to undertake the work. The architect was successful in both Stages 1 and 2. Regrettably nothing had been confirmed in writing at the appropriate time. The consortium offered the architect a pittance and engaged another much larger practice, without the design skills, to take the scheme forward.

Practices entering any competitions need to be aware of Rule 3.5 of the RIBA Code of Professional Conduct, which prevents an architect entering a competition declared unacceptable by the RIBA. Equally, competition entrants must read the small print of the entry conditions. In one recent competition the winner was required to sign away the copyright in exchange for a £2000 fee![1]

Note

1 *Building Design* 6 April 2001 p. 1.

11 What fees, and when will they be paid?

The *Architect's Handbook of Practice Management* says of profitability that:

> *it should be seen as a qualifiable target for the performance of the business overall, as a target for each job in its own right and for each fee-earning person employed by the practice.*[1]

It notes that 'profits can be eaten away by sloppy commissioning procedures', the tightening-up of which is a central purpose of this book.

SFA/99 gives four methods of charging fees, but whichever method is adopted, the practice must first know what it is going to cost the practice to undertake the commission. The financially successful practice is likely to be the one that gets this right, not least because most practices that make no profit do so because they have one, or probably more than one, seriously loss-making commissions. This happens time and again. Only time and effort taken to do the fee estimate properly at the right time will avoid this pitfall. The most accurate methods are:

- in-house records of what similar jobs have cost
- an assessment from first principles, using a project resource planning sheet or spreadsheet. The fee assessment needs to include anticipated expenditure in the following areas:
  - direct salaries
  - practice overhead additions to salaries, usually a known percentage
  - payments to contract staff
  - overtime payments
  - payments to sub-consultants
  - expenses
  - finance charges
  - allowance for inflation during the duration of the commission.

The estimated cost of providing the service can then be checked against the following published figures:

- the RIBA graphs published in *A Client's Guide to Engaging an Architect*[2]
- the annual survey published by Mirza and Nacey Research.[3] This document, although expensive, is particularly useful in that it gives data in the form of graphs based on 2000 jobs during the previous 12-month period 31 July to 30 June, showing percentage fees for projects of differing values in different sectors and using differing procurement methods. The graphs show an indicative *line of best fit*. Hourly rates charged for staff at various

levels in practices of various sizes, in different parts of the country, are also given

- the BCIS publication *Review of Consultants' Fees on Construction Projects*.[4] Unfortunately this publication lumps all the consultants' fees together, but it has some useful indicators, especially when a multidiscipline consultancy fee is being quoted.

Having ascertained what the project will cost the practice it is necessary to give some consideration as to how much the practice wants the commission in the light of:

- current workload
- technical and human resources available
- market conditions: in an overheated market staff are likely to leave and only be replaceable at higher salaries – in a quiet market staffing is not a problem
- the type and long-term potential of the client
- the size and type of the project
- the distance of the project from the architect's office
- the effects of the project on cashflow.

The RIBA publication *A Guide to RIBA Forms of Appointment 1999* states that whatever fee method is chosen 'it is a gamble'.[5] That is an unfortunate statement. Of course there is a risk in any job, but what is required is to undertake a risk assessment, so that the risks are appreciated and can be minimised. If there are any substantial risks that might cause insurmountable difficulties for the practice, the job should not be taken. Risks to be assessed include:

- key staff leaving
- key staff off with long-term illness, or maternity leave
- client difficulties, as discussed in Chapter 3, section 3.13
- client insolvency
- cash flow difficulties
- lack of experience, as discussed in Chapter 6, section 6.1
- tight timescales

and on the other side:

- likely additional fees in respect of variations, additional services, extensions of time etc.
- likelihood of repeat business.

When all the above has been done an adjustment needs to be made for a profit margin. This margin will assume that notional salaries have been allowed in respect of principals and directors. It will take into account how much the practice wants the work, the risks involved in undertaking it, and market conditions. Possibly a negotiating margin will be incorporated.

There may be occasions where it is appropriate to undertake work at or below the cost to the practice. This is a dangerous strategy but if, nine months through the financial year, the practice has made more than its budgeted profit and has no other work for the following three months, to go in at a figure below cost may make the difference between achieving the budgeted profit at the end of the year or making a loss.

Similarly, if the practice is very keen to get work in a particular sector or for a particular client, it may allocate part of its marketing budget to reducing fees for that project. But:

> *There is a point, however, below which the architect cannot give a satisfactory standard of service. To negotiate a fee below that point is commercial suicide to say nothing of being unprofessional... Although everyone in business must face commercial reality architects do the profession no favours by working for very low fees or for nothing at all.*[6]

It needs to be appreciated that fees can only be reduced by:

- reducing profit, which in most architectural practices is minimal
- reducing overheads, which is rarely feasible
- using lower-paid staff, which means less experienced staff
- cutting down the hours worked, which means something must go
- increasing efficiency, which most architects are striving to do

It has been said that the fee quoted should be the architect's price for the client's stated requirements at the outset, no more and no less. This may be so, but one commonly hears it said that 'everything is negotiable', and the purchasing departments of many client companies start from that position. So what does the architect do? Follow the puritan tradition of putting a price on his or her services, calculated on the basis of what the work will cost plus a fair profit? Or take the approach of the eastern bazaar, going in high with a margin to knock off to leave the price that is actually wanted? With the latter approach, if the commission is not lost, there is a chance of getting the superprofit on the higher price or pleasing the clients by leaving them thinking they have obtained a bargain! But what is a fair profit? It is entirely what the market will pay. Why can a solicitor command £200 an hour and a plumber only £15 (except of course over seasonal holidays when the plumber can command £50)? Most architects are likely to choose the former approach and go in at the lowest acceptable fee at which they can do the work, with negotiation restricted to such areas as:

- no additional fee for accepting the role of design team leader
- no additional fee for certain expenses
- adjustments to the stages at which payments are made
- extension of credit term on invoices (but not for too long!).

Any architect in private practice would do well to read some textbooks on negotiating, because the likelihood is that he or she will be across the table from someone who is experienced in it.

The following sections of Principle Three of the RIBA Code of Professional Conduct should be noted:

> ...*a member undertakes:*

> *3.3 When offering services as an independent consulting architect, not to revise a fee quotation to take account of the fee quoted by another architect for the same service.*

This is to prevent architects from undercutting each other's fee bids in a so-called 'Dutch auction' situation.

> *3.4 Not to attempt to oust another architect from an engagement.*

> *3.7 Not to maliciously or unfairly criticise or attempt to discredit another member or his work.*

Many hours are spent by practices in obtaining the opportunity to bid or submit project proposals. It follows that equal effort should then be made to manage the bid process. Too low a fee, too tight a programme, too vague a brief are the ingredients of disaster.

11.1 Percentage fees

This is the traditional, most convenient, most easily understood and most easily comparable method of charging. It also takes inflation and deflation into account, but perhaps too much so in that the construction industry is very much affected by changes in the economic climate such that:

- in times of recession building prices fall sharply, generally well in advance of professional salaries, thus reducing the architect's anticipated fee, possibly to a level that may cause embarrassment to the practice
- a fee based on 'construction cost' may give the architect an inflated return, particularly when there has been a gap between the time when working

drawings were prepared (that is, the most labour-intensive period of the architect's involvement) and actual construction on site.

- In long-term projects these possible anomalies can be catered for by basing the fees for each stage on the criteria for interim fee calculations given in SFA/99 at section 5.2.2:

  (a) Before tenders are obtained – the current approved estimate of the Construction Cost

  (b) After tenders have been obtained – the lowest acceptable tender

  (c) After the contract is let either the certified value or the anticipated final account.

The definition of construction cost on which a percentage fee is based can lead to difficulties. SFA/99 defines it as follows:

> *The Construction Cost shall be the latest estimate for or the actual cost of constructing and/or managing the construction of the project…*

The following are included in the construction cost:

> *Any contingency or design reserve cost allowance*

> *The cost as if new of any equipment provided or to be provided by the Client to a contractor for installation during construction of the project.*

The word 'equipment' is misleading. Besides client's equipment as such, it is presumably intended to cover materials supplied free of charge by the employer to the contractor. This is a relatively common occurrence:

Examples

A haulage company wanting a modest warehouse had purchased a steel portal frame from a demolition contractor who was clearing a nearby factory site, and instructed its architect to incorporate it into the new warehouse. The construction cost would be calculated on the basis that the supply and erection of a new portal frame was included. (In any event, with increased handling and preparation, the savings were likely to be considerably less than the employer envisaged!)

A client owned a site with outline planning permission for a house, but with a planning condition requiring it to be in the vernacular tradition of the area. For some time the client had been collecting second-hand stone, oak beams and stone roofing slabs. These were to be issued free to the contractor and incorporated into the building. The construction cost as defined by SFA/99 would include the 'cost as if new' of these materials if they fell within the description of 'equipment', but it would be prudent to define in the terms of engagement whether or not the construction cost was to include the cost of these materials as if they were new, or the second-hand cost of the materials.

A new church building was to incorporate a pipe organ that had been donated, free of charge, from an existing church building that was being demolished. The cost of a new organ of equivalent size would have been significantly in excess of the cost of moving the second-hand organ. If the organ had not been donated, the new church would probably have purchased a modest free-standing baroque organ, which would not have been part of the building contract.

Circumstances such as these can easily lead to misunderstanding, with resultant tension between architect and client or the architect being out of pocket. Both of these unwanted outcomes can be avoided by a little foresight, and by defining the position at an early stage.

Sometimes clients will wish to do some of the work themselves. The inference is that the cost of any such works will be part of 'the ascertained gross final cost of all works'. But SFA/99 is not as clear as it might be.

Examples

A client had an in-house maintenance department, largely painters. At the initial stage he instructed that all internal decorating be omitted from the building contract, to be done by his own labour once the main contractor had left site. Was the architect entitled to fees on the decorating?

In a large industrial warehouse the heating was to be by free-standing oil-fired blower heaters. The client's works engineer decided that he would look after the heating installation as a separate direct contract. Was the architect entitled to fees on the heating installation?

These points are important, and need to be defined at the outset, because, with architect's profit margins often well under 5%, what is included in or excluded from the construction cost can make the difference between profit and loss. If a significant amount of work is to be excluded, then the percentage fee will need to increase.

Clause 5.2.2 of SFA/99 states that where the client is the contractor, the final costs shall include an allowance for the contractor's profit and overheads. As the percentage for this allowance can vary widely, and may be difficult to ascertain, it would be prudent to include reference to specific percentages or lump sums at the outset.

The construction cost as defined by SFA/99 excludes:

- value added tax
- the design fees of any specialist for work on which consultants would otherwise have been employed
- any loss or expense payments payable to, or liquidated damages recoverable from, a contractor by a client. This is an important point, as traditionally some architects have claimed fees on loss and expense payments, taking the view that these fees reimburse the time spent in negotiating such payments. This is not the position taken by SFA/99, which omits fees on loss and expense payments but includes 'ascertainment of Contractor's claims' in Schedule 2: Services as an activity that will attract additional fees in accordance with Clause 5.6: that is, on a time basis.

Percentage fees have the great merit that the fees charged for projects of different types and sizes and by different procurement methods can be compared, and trends noted. For this reason, as well as convenience, percentages are likely to continue to be the basis on which fees are at least recorded for the foreseeable future.

A Client's Guide to Engaging an Architect includes graphs indicating *indicative percentage fee scales for normal services* for new works and works to existing buildings. In Figure 5 of that publication various building types are divided into five classifications. In general terms the more complex the building the higher the class number and the higher the percentage fee, which decreases as the construction cost increases.

11.2 Lump sum fees

SFA/99 gives two approaches to lump sum fees:

1. A lump sum based upon a stated percentage of the construction cost approved by the client at the end of Work Stage D, to be revised every 12 months in accordance with changes in the Retail Price Index, which is set out in Table 6.1 (all items) of *Labour Market Trends* published by the Office for National Statistics.
- Alternatively separate lump sums based on the stated percentage 'for each Work Stage based on the Construction Cost approved by the Client at the end of the previous stage'.
2. A fixed lump sum or sums, to be adjusted on a time basis 'if substantial amendments are made to the Brief and/or the Construction Cost and/or the Timetable' and again subject to adjustment every 12 months in accordance with the Retail Price Index.

Advice on lump sum fee arrangements is given in *A Guide to RIBA Forms of Appointment 1999* including the following:

- Predetermined lump sums are appropriate only when '…the scope of the project, the programme and cost are clearly defined from the outset and are likely to remain reasonably stable' or the service is to be provided is highly focused and to be undertaken over a very short period.
- In the case of commissions where changes are likely it may be appropriate 'to choose a method which can be used to calculate lump sums when the project has been sufficiently developed to fix scope, time and cost targets'.
- Other than in the cases indicated above, 'it is unwise to agree a fixed lump sum with no provision for variation (apart from movement in the Retail Price Index)'. On the contrary it is advisable 'to provide for the lump sum(s) to be varied if either of the parameters for time or cost is varied by more than (say 15%)'.[7]

11.3 Time charges

SFA/99 states at 5.4:

A time based fee shall be ascertained by multiplying the time reasonably spent in the performance of the Services by the relevant hourly rate set out in Schedule 3. Time 'reasonably spent' shall include the time spent in connection with performance of the Services in travelling from and returning to the Architect's office.

Clause 5.9 of SFA/99 further states:

The Architect shall maintain records of time spent on Services performed on a time basis, and of expenses and disbursements and shall make these available to the Client on reasonable request.

The hourly rates are to be set out in the Schedule to SFA/99 for categories of staff and/or named individuals. Clause 5.5, quoted above, applies the RPI to time charges. A method of calculating time charge rates is given in section B3 of the *Architect's Handbook of Practice Management*. Indicative hourly rates are given in Figure 4 of *A Client's Guide to Engaging an Architect*, and average fees charged for personnel at different levels and in different parts of the country during the preceding 12 months are given in Mirza and Nacey's annual survey. There is a wide spread of hourly rates, from the 'shocking figures' released by the RIBA in May 2001 indicating that 'some small practitioners are charging just £10 an hour for their services',[8] to the indicative rate of £180 per hour for a partner or equivalent undertaking specialist work, as given in *A Client's Guide to Engaging an Architect*.

There are few clients who will accept work on an hourly rate basis. The main exception is in dispute resolution, where hourly rates are the norm. Hourly rates are also appropriate for 'additional fees'. It is worth making the point that traditionally, once a percentage fee was agreed, an architect did not normally charge extras, but spoke instead of 'swings and roundabouts', and absorbed the costs of endless negotiations with tiresome planning officials, the cost of client variations, the bankruptcies of nominated subcontractors and the like. At that time there were fixed scale fees, and every architect had to charge them. Now, if architects are to be treated as any other contractor, those who survive in the competitive marketplace will be the practitioners who carefully specify the services that will be provided and charge for every variation or disruption over and above those services. Clause 5.6 of SFA/99 deals with this point, and states that if, for reasons beyond their control, architects are involved in extra work or incur extra expenses, they shall be entitled to charge for them on a time basis. Typical, but not exhaustive, reasons for such extra charges are listed as follows:

1. The Scope of the Services or the Timetable or the period specified for any Work Stage is varied by the Client.

2. The nature of the Project requires that substantial parts of the design cannot be completed or must be specified provisionally or approximately before construction commences.

3. The Architect is required to vary any item of work commenced or completed pursuant to the Agreement or to provide a new design after the Client has authorised the Architect to develop an approved design.

4. Delay or disruption by others.

5. Prolongation of any building contract(s) relating to the Project.

6. The Architect consents to enter into any third party agreement the form of beneficiary of which had not been agreed by the Architect at the date of the Agreement.

7. The cost of any work designed by the Architect or the cost of special equipment is excluded from the Construction Cost.

Thus it is essential that each team leader within the architect's office is alive to what has been quoted for and what constitutes 'extra work', and that the practice has a sophisticated time-recording system so that not only is time booked against the project, but, as soon as an 'extra work' item is identified, the time involved is allocated to that item and the client is advised.

11.4 Other methods of charging

There are other methods of charging, but they are rarely used. One example is the small housing developer who pays the architect on the basis of a lump sum per house, payable immediately the sale of the house is completed. In such a case the architect needs to take financing charges into account when calculating the appropriate fee.

Another method – in the high risk category – is for the architect to be rewarded by a proportion of the profit made by the development he or she has designed. But how is the profit to be quantified?

11.5 Expenses and disbursements

Clause 5.8 of SFA/99 states:

The Client shall reimburse at net cost plus the handling charge stated in Schedule 3:

1. Expenses specified in Schedule 3

2. Expenses other than those specified and incurred with the prior authorisation of the Client

3. Any disbursements made on the Client's behalf.

It is usual to charge for:

- prints of drawings
- plots of drawings
- mileage
- parking
- fares on public transport (air/train/taxi)
- subsistence
- overnight accommodation
- international telephones and postages
- courier services/special deliveries
- photocopies
- purchase of contract documents.

It is not usual to charge for:

- secretarial services
- UK telephone calls, faxes, postages
- e-mails.

Disbursements might include:

- *payment of planning fees*
- *payment of Building Regulation fees.* On any but very small projects for substantial clients, it is safer to ask the client to issue the appropriate cheque for these statutory payments.
- *payments to client-nominated sub-consultants.* This is a dangerous area. Even if a sub-consultant is client-nominated, the architect may be responsible for the sub-consultant's performance, and all the warnings set out in section 12.5 of Chapter 12 should be heeded, unless it is agreed in writing with all parties that the architect, in appointing the sub-consultant, is acting solely in the role of client's agent, and that the sub-consultant's contract is directly with the client.

11.6 Stage payments

The programming of interim payments will be influenced by the size and type of the project and commercial considerations, not least cash flow.

The RIBA's current recommendations, given in various publications, are listed in Table 11.1.

Table 11.1 Stage payments: RIBA current recommendations

Work stage	Percentage
C: Outline proposals	20%
D: Detailed proposals	20%
E: Final proposals	15%
F: Production information	20%
G: Tender documentation	2%
H: Tender action	1%
J: Mobilisation	1%
K: Construction	20%
L: After practical completion	1%
Total	100%

It is unlikely that Stage L can be billed immediately after practical completion; it will probably have to wait until after the end of the defects liability period, and the inspection of the making good of defects and issue of the final certificate, which in a large project may be years rather than months. In any work stage that is likely to go on for many weeks, some method of interim payment within that stage is likely to be appropriate, and indeed the Housing Grants, Construction and Regeneration Act 1996 (HGC&RA) requires it. On the basis of the above percentages the fee for perhaps all the pre-contract work stages may be split into monthly instalments. Traditionally the post-contract percentage is applied to the value of work certified. The important point that needs to be stated here is that arrangements should be agreed that allow for the invoicing of regular small sums (and they should then be invoiced promptly!). SFA/99 assists at Clause 5.10:

> The Architect's accounts shall be issued at intervals of not less than one month and shall include any additional fees, expenses or disbursements and state the basis of calculation of the amounts due.

> Instalments of the fees shall be calculated on the basis of the Architect's estimate of the percentage of completion of the Work Stage or other Services for such other method specified in Schedule 3.

11.7 Credit terms and interest

Clause 5.10 of SFA/99 also includes:

> Payments under the Agreement shall become due to the Architect on issue of the Architect's accounts. The final date for such payments by the Client shall be 30 days from the date of issue of an account.

Clause 5.13 deals with interest:

> Any sums due and remaining unpaid at the expiry of 30 days after the date of issue of an account from the Architect shall bear interest. Interest shall be payable at 8% over the Bank of England base rate current at the date of issue of the account.

Some clients may object to this. If so the appropriate response is to ask whether it is the client's intention to pay late, because – if not – any interest charge is irrelevant. It is also worth noting that this clause has the weight of the Late Payment of Commercial Debts (Interest) Act 1998 behind it.

Clause 5.12 of SFA/99 deals with the need for the client to serve written notice on the architect if intending to withhold payment of any part of an account, and to specify the ground or grounds. If the client does not do so, and does not pay, the architect may follow the provisions of the HGC&RA and suspend work. This is obviously a drastic remedy, and should be applied only with great caution. However, having said that, and notwithstanding the interest provisions, no prudent architect will let a client get away with late payments. Experience indicates that the longer an invoice is outstanding the harder it is to get it paid.

Further reading

*RICS/BCIS *Review of Consultants' Fees on Construction Projects* (BCIS, 2001).

*Davis, Langdon & Everest (eds.) *Spon's Architects' and Builders' Price Book* 125th edn (E & FN Spon, 2000; published annually). The 'Fees for professional services' section contains brief details of architects', quantity surveyors' and consulting engineers' indicative fee scales.

*S. Cox and A. Hamilton (eds) *Architect's Handbook of Practice Management* 6th edn, Chapter B3 (RIBA Publications, 1998).

*Mirza & Nacey Research *Architect's Fees: A Survey of the Fees Charged by Private Architectural Practices* (published annually).

A Client's Guide to Engaging an Architect (Including Guidance on Fees) rev. edn (RIBA Publications, 2000).

A Client's Guide to Engaging an Architect (Including Guidance on Fees): Small Works Only rev. edn (RIBA Publications, 2000).

Architect's Appointment: Historic Buildings – Repairs and Conservation Work (RIBA Publications, 1990).

A Guide to Painless Financial Management and Job Costing (Small Practices series) (RIBA Publications, 2000).

*R. Phillips (ed. S. Lupton and M. Lane) *The Architect's Contract: A Guide to RIBA Forms of Appointment 1999 and Other Architect's Appointments*, pp 38–41 (RIBA Publications, 1999).

Notes

1 S. Cox and A. Hamilton (eds) *Architect's Handbook of Practice Management* 6th edn, p 62 (RIBA Publications, 1998).

2 *A Client's Guide to Engaging an Architect (Including Guidance on Fees)* rev. edn (RIBA Publications, 2000).

3 Mirza & Nacey Research *Architect's Fees: A Survey of the Fees Charged by Private Architectural Practices* (published annually).

4 RICS/BCIS *Review of Consultants' Fees on Construction Projects* (BCIS, 2001).

5 R. Phillips (ed. S. Lupton and M. Lane) *The Architect's Contract: A Guide to RIBA Forms of Appointment 1999 and Other Architect's Appointments* (RIBA Publications, 1999).

6 D. Chappell and A. Willis *The Architect in Practice* 8th edn, p 95 (Blackwell Science, 2000).

7 *The Architect's Contract: A Guide to RIBA Forms of Appointment 1999 and Other Architect's Appointments*, p 39 (RIBA Publications, 1999).

8 *Building Design* 25 May 2001, p 3.

12 Working with other consultants

12.1 The traditional arrangement

Traditionally a client entered into direct contracts with each of several consultants whose expertise would be required for the project. This was accepted as the preferred norm by the various professional bodies, who were cautious about their members' taking on responsibilities for other consultants of whose disciplines they had only a superficial knowledge. It was also argued that it was in the interests of the client, particularly with regard to the role of the quantity surveyor, giving the client better cost control and preventing the inclusion of hidden contingencies or subsequent 'teaming and lading', which could occur if the quantity surveyor was employed by the architect or engineer.

Today there is a shift away from direct appointments, largely because when things go wrong there is a tendency for one consultant to blame another, and this can make it difficult for an employer to obtain redress. The move away from traditional contracting to design and build is also influenced by this point. In cases where consultants are all appointed separately, it is vital that the responsibilities of each consultant, both towards the client and towards each other, are clearly defined, and that one of them has a leadership role, be it as *project manager* or *designated lead consultant* or *design team leader*.

SFA/99 provides for other consultants and designers to be listed at Schedule 4.

Architects should insist on their right to check the terms of appointment and services of other consultants and, if necessary, ask for them to be changed. If the client disagrees, the architect should put a disclaimer of responsibility in writing. The terms under which consultants are appointed should state their responsibility for complying with the architect's requirements regarding time and programme.

12.2 The lead consultant

Traditionally the architect has acted as the *lead consultant* and *design team leader*, and if nothing is said there may well be a presumption that the architect has assumed these roles because this was traditionally the case and also because the architect's terms of engagement often involve some element of coordination.

Without someone having the responsibility for leadership of a number of independently appointed consultants there is a high risk of the project getting into difficulties. The discipline of the lead consultant does not matter; what *is* important is to get the right person. The arrangements should be written into the terms of engagement of all the consultants, and should be reflected in the fee level of the lead consultant, because the responsibility carried by the lead consultant is considerable, especially in:

- preparing a design stage programme
- monitoring compliance with the design stage programme
- chairing the design team meetings
- ensuring coordination between the various consultants' proposals.

It is in the area of coordination that the lead consultant is most vulnerable. The most serious coordination problems tend to occur in the following areas:

- size of plant rooms
- space for vertical and horizontal services, especially for air-handling ductwork
- headroom beneath downstand beams, especially in the vicinity of staircases.

A particular problem is that the M & E consultants are likely to be appointed on terms that require them to do schematic drawings only, leaving the appointed subcontractor to do all the detailed drawings, often at far too late a stage.

Another problem area is that of design work done by specialist subcontractors, nominated or named. Timescales and critical dates for their information must be incorporated into the design stage programme and the specialist subcontracts drawn accordingly.

Possible solutions to these problems are:

- for the M & E consultant to be engaged to do the full design, in the same way as the architect does for the fabric of the building. This will increase consultancy fees but should reduce the subcontractor's tender by the extent of the subcontractor's design fees; although this approach may be countered by the suggestion that it will increase the M & E tender because the consultant will not 'shop around' like a subcontractor who may be able to secure discounts. Nevertheless, there are very strong arguments in favour of full consultant design.
- for the M & E subcontractor(s) to be brought in at a very early stage on some form of negotiated two-stage basis, and for the subcontractor(s) to work closely with the architect in producing the M & E working drawings at the stage the architect needs them.

These approaches may, at first sight, cost slightly more, but any such increased sums are likely to be more than saved in the avoidance of variations when on site and subsequent disruption claims.

As with almost everything nowadays, good management and paperwork are essential and, so far as the lead consultant is concerned, this will include:

- preparation and issue of design stage programme, and updates
- issue of schedule of critical dates, unless these are shown on the programme
- convening, chairing and issuing minutes of regular design team meetings
- taking firm and decisive action if, and as soon as, it becomes clear that critical dates are not going to be met
- chairing, and issuing minutes of, site meetings
- making sure that information is issued to the contractor on time and that other contractual responsibilities are complied with by the consultant team
- handling the crises that from time to time afflict almost every construction project
- keeping the client advised, particularly when the project is in difficulties.

The formalisation of the design team leadership role is exemplified in the changes to the RIBA's recommended terms of engagement of architects as illustrated below. This draws attention to the increasing complexity of the leadership and coordination roles, which architects traditionally undertook as a matter of course.

The RIBA document *Architect's Appointment* (the 'blue book'), which set out the normal basis for engaging an architect until 1992, included '…coordinate and design work done by consultants, specialist contractors, subcontractors and suppliers…' but made no mention of 'lead consultant'.

SFA/92 did not use the word 'coordinate', but the architect was to 'provide information to, discuss proposals with and incorporate input of other consultants into scheme design/detail design…' and in addition there was reference to 'Conditions Specific to Appointment of Consultants and Specialists where Architect is Lead Consultant'. These included a very full coordination role for the architect, as the following clauses from SFA/92 indicate:

4.1.5 The Client shall appoint and give authority to the Architect as Lead Consultant in relation to all consultants however employed. The Architect shall be the medium of all communications and instruction between the Client and the consultants, coordinate and integrate into the overall design the services of the consultants, require reports from the consultants.

4.2.4 The Client shall give the authority to the Architect to coordinate and integrate the services of all Specialists into the overall design and the Architect shall be responsible for such coordination and integration.

SFA/99 sets out the position differently. It draws a new distinction between *design leader* and *lead consultant,* and the role in which the architect is to be engaged must be specified. The lead consultant role is further broken down into *pre-construction* and as *contract administrator.* The duties in each role are set out in the *Services Supplement,* and, as the only realistic way in which the differently defined roles can be understood is to compare the definitions, they are quoted verbatim:

As Design Leader

The Architect has authority and responsibility for:

1. Directing the design process

2. Coordinating design of all constructional elements, including work by any Consultants, Specialists or Suppliers.

3. Establishing the form and content of design outputs, their interfaces and verification procedure.

4. Communicating with the Client on significant design issues.

As Lead Consultant (Pre-Construction)

The Architect has authority and responsibility in the pre-construction Work Stages for:

1. Coordinating and monitoring design work

2. Communications between the Client and the Consultants; except that communications on significant design matters are dealt with as design leader

3. Advising on the need for and the scope of services by Consultants, Specialists, Subcontractors or Suppliers

4. Advising on methods of procuring construction

5. Receiving regular status reports from each Consultant, including the design leader

6. Developing and managing change control procedures, making or obtaining decisions necessary for time and cost control

7. Reporting to the Client as appropriate.

As Lead Consultant and Contract Administrator

The Architect has authority and responsibility in the tender and construction Work Stages A–G for:

1. Inviting and appraising a tender or tenders including:…

2. Administering the building contract, including:…

3. Coordinating and monitoring the work of Consultants and Site Inspectors, if any, to the extent required for the administration of the building contract, including:…

4. Communications between the Client and the Consultants

5. Reporting to the Client as appropriate

It is not easy to distinguish between design leader and lead consultant. The roles obviously overlap. What is important is not so much the names but the functions. Any architect on any project must ensure that there is a person (or firm) clearly appointed to provide leadership of the design team, and that the extent and responsibilities of that leadership are defined and reflected in the fees agreed.

12.3 The project manager

Rather than having a lead consultant, the responsibility for leading the design team (and far wider responsibilities) may be vested in a project manager. Alternatively there may be both a lead consultant and a project manager.

There is a real difficulty here in that the term 'project manager' has just about as many definitions as there are project managers. Examples include the following.

- The project manager who is a member of the employer's in-house staff, or whose services are engaged for the project and who is charged with getting the project completed on time etc. The project manager may be a construction professional, or the traditional works engineer, or the maintenance manager or the estates bursar or an administrator, or the employer in person. Such a person is often invaluable for providing a single point of contact with the client but is usually not appropriate to undertake the role of lead consultant, which should remain with one of the design team.

- The project manager as employed in the building surveying sections of some of the large firms of commercial estate agents, which see the offering of this 'service' as an additional source of fee income. Such project managers are likely to major on the terms of engagement of the design team, warranties and contractual arrangements, and may also deal with the funding or subsequent letting or sale of the development. They appear to be masters of risk-shunting (from themselves) and to take a healthy fee for doing so. A lead consultant is still likely to be required.
- The project manager as named in the Engineering and Construction Contract or GC/Works/1 contract, and who is similar to the traditional resident engineer.
- The project manager who uses the title as a synonym for lead consultant.
- The project manager who actually manages the construction of the project and is responsible for the letting of the various works package contracts under management contracting, construction management or design and build procurement systems.
- Various combinations of the above.

If undertaking a commission where there is to be a project manager it is essential to ascertain the extent and limits of that person's role and authority. Equally, if an architect is going to hold him or herself out for appointment as project manager, it is essential to spell out:

- exactly what work will be done within that role
- even more importantly, what it does not cover
- the powers and duties of the project manager relating to other consultants
- the powers and duties of the project manager relating to contractors.

The RIBA form of appointment of a project manager was briefly referred to in section 9.7 of Chapter 9, where it is noted that the project manager's services, as defined, are little more than those of a lead consultant. It is nevertheless more satisfactory than the equivalent and better-known RICS document, with which any architect offering project management services should also be conversant.

12.4 Recommending and appointing other consultants

Traditionally the architect was invariably appointed first and assembled a consultant team with the client. Those days have to some extent gone, and it may be the quantity surveyor or structural engineer who is appointed first. Nevertheless there are still many occasions when the architect is asked to recommend other consultants. It is unwise to do so.

If an unsuitable consultant is recommended and does not perform, the architect may be held liable for that consultant's failure. The answer is to put forward names of firms with a good track record with buildings of the size and type in hand, saying no more than, 'Here are names of firms well known in the specific field' or '…whom I have found to be reliable'. Recommendations that are made merely on the grounds of personal connections, or because of the hope or promise of reciprocal recommendations, are particularly to be avoided.

On occasion the client may ask the architect to appoint other consultants on the client's behalf. When this occurs there are two particular points to watch:

- that the wording of any letter of appointment, or similar document, spells out very clearly that the architect, in appointing the other consultant, is acting as agent for and on behalf of the client, and that it will be the client with whom the consultant has a contact and to whom the consultant's invoice must be rendered
- that copies of the consultant's terms of engagement are sent to the client, preferably for approval prior to appointment, so that there can be no future misunderstanding.

If these steps are not taken there is a risk that if the client declines to pay the other consultants, or goes into liquidation, the consultants will look to the architect for payment of their fees.

12.5 Sub-consultants

There is an increasing tendency for clients to want to deal with one consultant only, and to look for a fee quotation covering all the required disciplines. A primary motive for this is to avoid split responsibility if things go wrong. If the employer's contract is going to be with the architect for all the consulting services, the vital point to note is that the architect will be responsible to the client for the work of any sub-consultants, and for any failures in that work.

There is always a higher risk when one is providing a service that is not within one's primary discipline. As with most other things, clear documentation between all parties is essential. Important points to watch include the following:

- that the services referred to in the architect's offer to the client are identical to those offered to the architect by the sub-consultant. There must be a back-to-back agreement, with no gap between duties owed by the architect and those owed to the architect. The simplest way of achieving this is to have a clause rehearsing the architect's head appointment contract and annexing that contract (with any sensitive details about total remuneration excised) to each sub-consultancy agreement

- that there are no obvious omissions from the schedule of work proposed by the sub-consultant that will allow him or her to charge additional fees, which it may be difficult to pass on to the client
- that if the architect's contract is by way of a deed, so is the sub-consultancy contract
- that the sub-consultant carries sufficient professional indemnity insurance. This may be difficult to achieve in some instances: for example, there may be some restriction on the extent to which an engineering sub-consultant can obtain PII for pollution or contaminated land matters. Any such restriction must be passed on by the architect in the main agreement, otherwise the architect will find an unrestricted obligation to maintain insurance for all matters but will be unable to secure the necessary cover from the engineer
- that the architect's professional indemnity insurance will extend to the work undertaken by the sub-consultant in the event of the sub-consultant's insurance lapsing. This is a real possibility in that insurance cover is normally related to the date a claim is made, and it may be that by the time things go wrong, up to 12 years after practical completion with a deed or 15 years from the breach of duty in tort, the sub-consultant is no longer trading and hence not insured
- that the sub-consultant has sufficient 'wool on his back'. It is not unknown for professional practices that are limited liability companies to go into liquidation
- that the architect does not allow extended credit to the client, because the architect will be responsible for the sub-consultants' bills and will still be responsible if the client refuses to pay for some reason or goes into liquidation. Traditionally there was some comfort in 'pay when paid' clauses, but these are no longer possible following the legislation contained in the Housing Grants, Construction and Regeneration Act 1996. Engaging sub-consultants is a high-risk activity for an architect.

A sub-consultant may undertake the work in his or her own name, as if under a traditional form of appointment, or may 'ghost' and do the work in the name of the architect's practice. The former is generally to be preferred.

12.6 Sub-letting work

From time to time practices may need help at critical stages on large projects, and will look to other practices to provide assistance. This assistance will often be no more than the provision of labour-only drafting or CAD operation. However, it may be for a complete package of drawings, for a site survey, for clerk of works services or, where a small job is a long way from the office, for post-contract site visits. As usual the arrangements must be documented. The following are points to watch:

- Does the architect's professional indemnity insurance extend to labour-only subcontractors? Is this still the case if the subcontractor is a limited liability company and is producing a complete package of drawings, or undertaking a site survey, or making periodic inspections?
- Where a specific service is being provided by another established practice or firm, it is most important to ensure that it has indemnity insurance covering what it has contracted to do.
- Drawings prepared by sub-consultants should be checked very carefully.

There is another area of concern. The *RIBA Code of Professional Conduct* at 1.5 requires a Member 'not to transfer his responsibilities, or reduce the scope of services by subcontracting, without the prior consent of his client or without defining the changes in the responsibilities of those concerned'.

Practices may not wish their clients to know that they are under pressure. The line between seeking drafting help from another, perhaps one-man, practice and subcontracting a commission is a blurred one. The former is no different from employing contract staff, which is done on a widespread scale, but the latter clearly needs the client's approval.

12.7 Working as a sub-consultant

Much of what has been said above applies in the reverse situation. As usual, it is important to get everything documented and, as when working for a design and build contractor, to appreciate that the immediate client is not the end-user. There is of course a duty to the end-user, such as any architect has to those who will use the buildings but, notwithstanding any warranties given and any potential tortious liabilities to the building owner, the architect's primary duty is to the client – who in this case is the main consultant. Key points to bear in mind in this scenario include the following:

- What relationship does the sub-consultant have with the building owner or the building owner's project manager? Are all communications with these parties to be through the sub-consultant's client – that is, through the main consultant?
- Is the consultant client financially stable? Similarly, is the consultant client's own client financially stable?
- Does the consultant client have appropriate professional indemnity insurance?
- Has the consultant client got a formal agreement with the main client, incorporating the same terms as in the sub-consultancy contract?

12.8 The joint venture

One way of getting over the problem of being responsible for sub-consultants' fees in the event of the failure of the client is to form a joint venture consultancy for the commission. If this is done the documentation must set out the responsibilities of each party, and the basis on which individual members of the joint venture share the fees received and bear any losses that may be incurred. The writer's experience of joint venture consultancy is good: a separate limited liability company was set up and each participating practice nominated one director to the board of that company, which had its own bank account and took out its own professional indemnity insurance.

12.9 The clerk of works or site inspector

At one time it was usual to refer to the architect as 'supervising the contract', and local authority contracts referred to 'the supervising officer'. Given the dictionary meaning of supervision as 'to have general oversight' this was entirely reasonable. But, as in so many areas of life, the lawyers got hold of it and supervision came to mean 'constant oversight': thus *Architect's Appointment* (1982) omits any reference to supervision and defines the architect's duty as to *'visit the site as appropriate to inspect generally the progress and quality of work'*. The constant oversight or supervision was left to the resident clerk of works. But it has not stopped there: and the wording of SFA/99 has changed to 'K1 Make Visits to the Works in connection with the Architect's design' and no longer is the clerk of works to be described as providing 'supervision'. The clerk of works now makes 'inspections' (and indeed the old and respected, if misleading, title of *clerk of works* appears to be on its way out, to be replaced by the characterless but correct *site inspector*). Nowadays it is said that only the contractor provides 'supervision', and no prudent architect will use the term other than with reference to the contractor.

Traditionally the clerk of works was engaged and paid for by the client but was under the direction of the architect. The clerk of works carries a lot of responsibility, and the benefit to the architect of the clerk of works being employed by the client is that the client is vicariously liable for the performance of the clerk of works, thus reducing the architect's potential liability for damages.

Increasingly site inspectors are being provided by specialist consultancies, and where such a consultancy is engaged by the client section 3.11 of SFA/99 will be relevant:

The Client, in respect of any work or services in connection with the Project performed or to be performed by any person other than the Architect, shall:

1. Hold such a person responsible for the competence and performance of his services and for visits to the site in connection with the work undertaken by him.

This of course will not apply if the site inspector is a sub-consultants of the architect.

Section 2.5 of SFA/99 makes the architect responsible for advising the client on the need for the appointment of full-or part-time site inspectors. A prudent architect will:

- always give advice on this point
- never say that a site inspector is unnecessary because the architect 'will make a few more visits and keep an eye on it'
- always point out to the client the need to make a considered risk assessment taking into account the fact that reducing the extent (and hence the cost) of site inspection will increase the risk of defects being undetected.

Section 3.10 of SFA/99 states:

Where it is agreed Site Inspectors shall be appointed they shall be under the direction of the Lead Consultant and the Client shall appoint and pay them under separate agreements and shall confirm in writing to the Architect the services to be performed, their disciplines and the expected duration of their employment.

This is the ideal and the norm, but there will be occasions when the architect is required to provide a composite service including site inspection, either by site inspectors on the architect's own staff or by way of sub-consultancy to an individual or firm providing site inspection services. In such circumstances the architect becomes responsible for the work of the site inspectors: that is, overlooking and checking the work, usually throughout each working day. Points to watch, when the clerk of works or site inspector is employed by or is a sub-consultant to the architect, include the following:

- The architect's professional indemnity insurance must extend to covering the employee clerk of works' services.
- If the clerk of works' services are provided by a firm as a sub-consultant, the architect must ensure that that firm has adequate indemnity insurance, and that if in the future that insurance lapses, the work will be covered by the architect's own professional indemnity insurance.
- The architect needs to be aware that a traditional clerk of works, typically from a joinery background, is unlikely to have the skills to inspect some parts of the works, including structural concrete work, specialists' cladding and

particularly the complex M & E services, and therefore an appropriate limitation may be needed in the architect's terms of engagement relating to site inspection and/or the client must be given appropriate advice.

- If the architect does not have an in-house M & E engineer, or some formal arrangement with an M & E engineer, it is folly to take on the responsibility for the inspection of M & E work. If that work subsequently does not function properly, the architect is likely to be sucked into the ensuing litigation and may well face something like 25% responsibility if there was inadequate inspection, rising to 100% if other parties are in liquidation – and the architect's professional indemnity insurance may not extend to inspection of M & E work. If the faulty installation causes a fire the consequential losses could be enormous.

Example
A flue from a stand-by generator passed through the roof of a new large office complex. When the generator was tested just before practical completion the roof timbers caught fire because the flue insulation had been omitted. The insurers paid out and subsequently sued the architect, the M & E consultant and the M & E subcontractor who joined in the generator sub-subcontractor who joined in the flue sub-sub-subcontractor. Who was responsible?

Further reading

RICS/BCIS *Review of Consultants' Fees on Construction Projects* (BCIS, 2001).

CIOB *Code of Practice for Project Management for Construction and Development* 2nd edn (Longman, 1996).

NJCC *Guidance Note 1: Joint Venture Tendering for Contracts in the United Kingdom* rev. edn (NJCC, 1996).

S. Reiss *Project Management Demystified* 2nd edn (E & FN Spon, 1995).

The Architect's Contract: A Guide to RIBA Forms of Appointment 1999 and other Architect's Appointments (RIBA Publications, 1999).

S. Cox and A. Hamilton (eds) *Clerk of Works Manual* 3rd edn (RIBA Publications, 1994).

*Davis, Langdon & Everest (eds) *Spon's Architects' and Builders' Price Book* 125th edn (E & FN Spon, 2000; published annually). See section on 'Fees for professional services'.

13 Design by nominated or named subcontractors

JCT98 makes provision for nominated subcontractors and IFC98 for named subcontractors. There has been a marked move away from nomination during the last decade because of the considerable contractual difficulties to which it can lead. For example, the financial failure of a nominated subcontractor part way through a contract can be a nightmare, leading to the need to re-nominate, inevitable delays and increased costs, some of which are likely to end up being paid by the employer. It is important to note that JCT98 does not have provision for named subcontractors, nor IFC98 for nomination.

There is often a need to involve specialist subcontractors in design, and the important point from the architect's position is to ensure that the architect does not end up carrying responsibility for that design, nor for any delays caused by late information from the designing subcontractor. To put in place necessary safeguards the following procedures are appropriate:

- The architect should use the standard JCT documentation for nominated or named subcontractors and in particular ensure that design warranties in favour of the employer are in place when the contracts are let; later may be too late!
- The architect should ensure that the employer is aware that design work is being done by specialist subcontractors and has agreed to such delegation by the architect. There is provision for these specialist subcontractors to be listed at Schedule 4 of SFA/99, and Clause 2.4 of SFA/99 requires the architect to:
  ...advise the Client on the appointment of Consultants or other persons, other than those named in Schedule 4, to design and/or carry out certain parts of the Works or to provide specialist advice if required in connection with the Project.

If the proper documentation is not used and things go wrong, the architect may be in difficulties for delegating some of the design work to a specialist without the client's approval, or for failing to ensure that proper paperwork was in place to safeguard both the client and the architect. This includes excluding responsibility for parts of the building designed by others including specialist subcontractors. In *Baxell v Sheard Walshaw* (2000) the architect was found liable to a user of a building whose goods suffered damage caused by the defective design of a roof drainage system despite the fact that the detailed design work had been undertaken by a specialist subcontractor. See Chapter 8 on warranties.

Further reading

D. Chappell *Understanding JCT Standard Building Contracts* 6th edn (E & FN Spon, 2000).

14 All change

14.1 Client change

An architect's client is the person, persons or company with whom the architect enters into an agreement. It is not unusual for clients to undergo some form of change part way through a commission. Examples might include the following:

- A married or cohabiting couple for whom the architect is designing a new home separate because of the stress of the project. It is vital to get an agreement recorded with both of the partners as to who is going to continue to act as client and to give instructions.
- A client company changes its name or, worse, ceases to exist and a new company is formed with a similar name. The architect should must have letters on file confirming the position and should not be left working for a company that has no assets.
- The client company is taken over. This may be a problem if the new owners have a favourite architect whom they want to bring in.
- The client company goes into receivership, but the receiver wishes the work to continue. This may be a time for some hard bargaining: although the receiver will be responsible for fees incurred for work done on his instructions, the architect will remain an ordinary creditor in respect of work already invoiced. Thus an attempt should be made to negotiate the fee arrangement with the receiver to cover the potential losses.
- The composition of a partnership changes: for example a group of doctors building a new surgery, or solicitors refurbishing their offices. The architect's contract may need amendment to reflect this.
- A design and build contractor for whom the architect is working, or to whom the architect has been novated, may go into liquidation or have its contract terminated: another contractor appointed to complete the works may want the same architect to continue. In this case a new contract with the new contractor is necessary, and considerable caution is needed here as experience shows that building work undertaken by a contractor in financial difficulties is rarely correctly executed; the architect does not want to be left holding the howling baby.

In each case the important point is that the change is documented and the architect is satisfied that the new employer has the resources to pay and hopefully takes responsibility for monies due from any previous employer.

The above situations are relatively simple. Those that follow include some rather more complicated changes.

14.2 Sold with the building

It sometimes happens that a building on which an architect has worked or is working changes hands, and the architect goes with it! For example, the architect may have prepared designs and obtained planning permission for the conversion of a warehouse or office building into flats. The building is sold on the open market with the benefit of the planning approval. The purchaser may well decide to engage the architect who has done the work and already has knowledge of the building. This is a totally new commission, which will need a totally new agreement with the new client. Anything agreed with the previous client will be of no consequence without appropriate documentation. Fees owing by the previous client will be of no concern to the new client. However, it is likely that the new client has relied on the design work done for the previous client, and thus there may be a tortious liability to the new client in respect of the design work.

14.3 Consultant switch

An architect having been engaged by an employer to prepare initial designs for a design and build contract may not be retained as employer's representative, but could be re-employed by the successful contractor. This is not novation but is generally known as *consultant switch*. The contractor does not become responsible for the earlier design work undertaken by the architect for the employer. This arrangement needs the approval of the employer, the termination of the architect's contract with the employer, and the entering into completely new terms of engagement with the contractor. It is not without risks of misunderstanding and conflict, although it may avoid some of the pitfalls of novation referred to below. Careful drafting of the new terms of engagement is vital.

14.4 Novation

The original concept of design and build was just that: each contractor would submit a design and price – a *package deal*. A particular attraction of design and build to an employer is the one-stop responsibility. A number of employers, however, want to keep their hands on the design and are tempted to use design and build contracting as a method of transference of risk. There are also considerable difficulties in design and build if the planning permission situation is anything other than the most straightforward. Thus some clients have engaged architects, or even a complete design team, to progress the design in considerable detail, incorporated it into the employer's requirements, and then novated the design team to the chosen design and build contractor with one or more of the following points in mind:

- The employer wants to ensure that the design and build contractor becomes responsible for the total design. The architect, if novated, ceases to be the client's architect and becomes the contractor's architect. More importantly, it is as if this situation had always applied. The architect is liable to the contractor for all the design. This is, on the face of it, an attractive proposition for the employer, as the contractor may thus be required to accept total liability for the design. That is, the contractor takes responsibility for the work that the designers have already done as well as the work they will do, except where limited by contract such as by clause 2.1 of WCD98, which requires the contractor merely to 'complete the design'.
- The employer does not want to pay for consultancy services for contracts that do not get off the ground, and therefore seeks to engage the architect on an at-risk basis until the commission actually goes ahead on site, when all the architect's fees will become the responsibility of the design and build contractor.
- The employer, wholly incorrectly, sees novation as a means of keeping some ongoing control in the design, or even putting a 'mole' in the contractor's camp.
- The employer may believe that novation will avoid duplication of fees in that the contractor will not have to engage another architect to study and verify the pre-contract designs that form part of the employer's requirements.

Only the most compelling commercial reasons will motivate an architect to do more than initial design drawings on an 'at-risk' basis.

Novation is a risky business for an architect. The risks can be reduced by ensuring that there are proper agreements in place between the architect and the employer setting out, inter alia:

- a schedule of the pre-contract services to be provided
- a schedule of the post-contract services to be provided
- the wording of the warranty that the employer will almost certainly require in respect of both the pre-contract and post-contract services
- the fees to be paid, by whom and at what stages
- the timescale within which various services will be provided
- the timing at which novation will take place
- the reliance that the contractor can place on pre-tender design work
- the general terms of engagement
- the level of professional indemnity insurance cover
- dispute resolution procedure.

All this detail about the architect's package of services, terms of appointment etc.

will need to be incorporated into the employer's requirements so that there are no misunderstandings.

There are many downsides for an employer in novation, including the following:

- The employer does not get the benefit of the contractor's experienced in-house or preferred design team.
- So far as fees are concerned, the design and build contractor's in-house designers may be more competitive.
- The contractor can always override the input of a sub-consultant, and thus the employer may not be getting the control over the design that they think they are getting.
- If disputes arise, the employer will need all the friends they can get. Although the architect's professional duty is a wide one, the primary loyalty must be to the client and, once the architect is novated, the client is the contractor.
- If the contractor does not have liability for pre-contract design errors, any defect is likely to be the subject of expensive litigation to establish whether the error was pre- or post-contract.
  Example. A dispute having arisen between the employer and the contractor, the employer asked the novated architect to provide copies of relevant documents. The architect quite properly advised that she could not do so without the approval of her contractor client, which was not forthcoming.
- The architect has very different obligations when working for the contractor rather than the employer. The employer is interested in quality, function, aesthetics, time and price. The contractor is interested in profit. It is not easy, and sometimes it is impossible, to changes one's professional objectives to suit a change of paymaster. David Mosey writes:

  Novation confuses the normal lines of communication, and as a result they make it difficult for novated designers to behave with the required objectivity and professionalism.[1]

In general, novation is something to be avoided and something to advise clients against, for the reasons indicated above. The architect who has undertaken the original designs should be best placed to prepare the employer's requirements and act as employer's agent under a design and build contract. This is likely to be far more satisfactory to all parties. It will also help the architect to avoid the following specific risks:

- The contractor tenders against the architect's preliminary drawings and subsequently finds that the architect has not included for significant areas of work such as:
  - the provision of adequate fire escape routes

- the provision of pumped drainage
- the provision of an adequately sized plant room.

The contractor loses a lot of money on these items. This is why the employer has gone down the risk-shifting design and build route, as otherwise each of these points might have put the contractor into a claim situation. The architect could be a 'sitting duck' if the documentation is poor.

- In a normal design and build situation the drawings within the employer's requirements are likely to be described as schematic only, with a requirement for the contractor to be responsible for the design in every way. When there is novation the situation may be different. Schematic drawings only they may have been, but to what extent could the contractor reasonably have relied upon 'his architect' to have got the schematics right, especially if this is a case where the employer has had the architect do quite detailed drawings for incorporation into the employer's requirements and used (or misused?) the design and build system to transfer risk? It may be a very grey area.

  Example. An architect acting for the employer was asked to amplify the employer's requirements with a drainage layout during tender stage. He did so, and the contractor relied on that drawing in the preparation of his tender. The architect was subsequently novated, and on site it was found that the drainage layout was unworkable. The necessary variations significantly increased the drainage costs, which, because of the wording of the employer's requirements, were not recoverable from the employer. The architect, now novated, was sued by his contractor client.

- There is the problem that, once the contractor's tender has been accepted, the contractor is going to want drawings at an impossible speed. No doubt the employer will have messed about for months if not years and now seeks to make up some of that lost time by imposing the tightest possible programme on the contractor. This will almost certainly mean that the work has to commence without Building Regulations approval, and the novated architect will be in further difficulties when it is subsequently found that hastily prepared post-contract details do not comply with Building Regulations or meet the whims of a particular building inspector or fire officer.

'Clever' lawyers have come up with variants to novation, including:

- *partial novation*, where the unfortunate architect is on the one hand finalising work on designs on behalf of the design and build contractor and on the other hand monitoring the implementation of those designs for the employer
- *double novation*, where the architect is novated from the employer to the contractor upon the award of the contract, but only to practical completion, whereupon the architect is re-novated to the employer.

It is the almost universal opinion of construction professionals that such arrangements are recipes for disaster, and are to be avoided even more than straightforward novation. A construction lawyer writes:

> I must however counsel real caution to those who believe that they can marry just the good features of the (D&B) contract, and leave the other features on the shelf – either by providing the design to the Contractor, by making substantial amendment to the standard forms of contract, or by sophisticated novations or other tricks. I suspect that they do not really want design/build at all, and would be much better advised to return to traditional contracts.[2]

As a final warning, when the architect has changed horses, there will still be a tortious liability to the owner of the first horse if that owner can show reasonable reliance upon a negligent misstatement of the architect, and in certain respects the responsibility may be wider. Thus in a 1998 case architects employed by a design and build contractor were found to owe a duty of care in tort to the contractor's client and to the client's tenants, and a duty to advise both in respect of 'defects actually observed' by the architects in carrying out site inspections, irrespective of their contractual obligations.[3]

14.5 Taking over from another architect

There are many occasions when one architect takes over from another including:

- when a solo practitioner retires, becomes incapacitated or dies. A new contract with the employer, incorporating the new architect's terms and conditions, is necessary, and it is particularly important that the following are covered:
  - the work stages that the new architect is to undertake
  - the responsibility for the work previously done by the original architect
  - that there are no copyright issues in respect of drawings
- when another architect's engagement has been terminated or the architect has resigned. There are many reasons why an architect's engagement may be terminated, or an architect resigns – some good, some bad. The more usual include the following:
  - The architect fails to meet deadlines.
  - The employer does not like the architect's initial design or budget.
  - The M & E consultant has not performed, and the architect gets caught up because of his or her role in coordination or as lead consultant.
  - The building contract gets out of control – that is, it is late and subject to claims, or there is defective work.
  - There is a fall-out about fees for additional services.

- There are clashes of personality.
- The employer is utterly impossible.
- The employer does not pay bills.
- The employer wants the architect to do something that is unprofessional, or possibly even dishonest or fraudulent.
- The quality of work achieved is not what the employer was expecting.
- The building does not work as the employer expected it to.
- There are defects, and the builder is dilatory about sorting them out, or advises that they are design defects.
- The architect's service was below a reasonable standard.
- The architect has ceased trading, because he or she is in bankruptcy, in liquidation or in jail.

To take over a job from another practice is to step into a high-risk area. It is vital that terms of engagement are set out with clarity. Particular problem areas may be:

- *Obtaining documents.* This can be a serious problem if the client and the former architect are in contention, with fees unpaid and the original architect claiming a lien on the documents until payment is made. The new agreement must place the responsibility for providing full documentation with the client. If full files are not to hand, the new architect will be well advised to record this and refuse to be responsible for any matters that could not reasonably be foreseen but which might come to light when documents are eventually produced. It may be that when files are handed over they have been 'filleted'.
- *Copyright issues.* The original architect will hold the copyright of the design and the drawings, and must give approval before they can be reproduced. However, once the original architect is paid off, the client is likely to be free to use the drawings. A problem may occur, and the job be held up, if the original architect is claiming a lot of money for wrongful termination for breach of contract leading to loss of opportunity and profit. In such circumstances the client should be advised to engage a construction lawyer.
- *Responsibility for inspection of works to date.* The new architect must include a disclaimer stating that he or she has not inspected, and hence cannot be responsible for detecting any defects in, work that is covered, unexposed or inaccessible. The disclaimer might also specify that specialist examinations of work already done have not been included for, such as CCTV surveys of drains, laboratory tests of concrete, plaster, mortar etc., thermographic surveys to determine whether there are no gaps in cavity insulation, the taking of core samples to determine the thickness of road surfacing, excavating trial holes to determine the depth of foundations, or such other matters as are relevant to the particular building.
- *Responsibility for certification to date.* The two risk areas here are first that, where there is no quantity surveyor, the original architect has over-valued the

works, and second that he or she has failed to make adequate deductions for defective work. Again a disclaimer might be appropriate.

- *Adequacy of the design.* It may be appropriate for the new architect to take responsibility for checking the drawings and specification and reporting inadequacies to the client, provided fees are agreed to cover this onerous work.
- *Delays.* The new architect will need to exclude responsibility or delays, and loss and expense claims flowing therefrom, that have been caused or are likely to be caused by such things as:
  - the original architect's having failed to provide the contractor with the necessary drawings and other information promptly
  - the drawings and other documents not being readily available for issue because the original architect has a lien on them or there are copyright issues
  - the original architect's being well behind with the drawing programme, such that the new architect cannot reasonably catch up in time to prevent delays
  - delays caused by the changeover of architects: under most forms of contract it is incumbent on the employer to appoint a new architect if the services of the original architect are terminated.

Another area for the new architect to consider is the implications of issuing a Certificate of Practical Completion for a contract of which 95% has been administered by someone else.

Example

A large national contractor, known to be prone to making claims, submitted a large claim following the refurbishment of a city centre office block, largely blaming the architect for inadequate and late information. The architect would not grant the requested extension of time or agree the loss and expense claim. The very experienced developer client, in order to avoid arbitration, did a deal with the contractor over the head of the architect. The architect resigned. Unfortunately, although the pre-Practical Completion snag list had been prepared, the Certificate of Practical Completion had not been issued, and the issue of that certificate was the trigger in the developer's funding contract for the release of substantial funds. Under JCT80 it was necessary for the employer to formally terminate the engagement of the original architect and to appoint a new architect. The new architect prudently agreed terms that his responsibilities would not extent beyond checking that the items on the previously published snagging lists had been attended to and issuing the Certificate of Practical Completion, and that in particular he would not be responsible for design errors or defective materials and workmanship, beyond the checking of the snag lists.

Before undertaking any work the new architect will need to be assured that the former architect's employment has been properly terminated and the contractor advised. The new architect will need to notify the former architect of his or her involvement as a matter of courtesy and in order to comply with the RIBA Code of Professional Conduct, at 3.8:

> On being approached to undertake work upon which he knows or can ascertain by reasonable enquiry that another architect has an engagement with the same client, to notify the fact to such architect.

So often in these cases the project, for one reason or another, is in a chaotic state, and often the paperwork will be anything but in order. The new architect's fees should allow for this.

There is one situation where it may not be necessary to notify the existing or former architect. This is when matters appear to be going wrong and the new architect is instructed to investigate the situation and advise the employer on what to do and whether there may be redress against any of the parties: that is, in circumstances where the employer is considering legal proceedings. It is normally better if instructions in this circumstance come from the employer's solicitors. One reason for this is that any reports prepared in contemplation of possible litigation will not be disclosable if sent to the solicitor whereas, if commissioned by the employer, an initial report may well be disclosable in the event of subsequent litigation. The RIBA Code of Professional Conduct states at 3.9:

> When engaged to give an opinion on the work of another architect, to notify the fact to that architect unless it can be shown to be prejudicial to prospective or actual litigation to do so.

In such circumstances it is normally the case that notification will be prejudicial to prospective litigation. If in doubt, written guidance on this point should be sought from instructing solicitors.

In cases where litigation does ensue, it is quite likely that there will be contracts for remedial works to be administered, possibly by the architect who is advising in connection with the litigation. In such cases, if a final certificate has not been issued or the engagement of the former architect has not been formally terminated, the former architect will need to be notified.

Ideally, where a new architect takes over from another architect there needs to be a formal termination agreement between the former architect and the employer covering extent of responsibility, fees to be paid and copyright issues. This rarely happens, not least because the parties are often in dispute by this stage, but in any event there should be a formal letter of termination from one of the parties to the other. And the agreement with the new architect should take into account all that is said not just in this chapter but in this book!

14.6 Architect's in-house change

The parties to a contract change only if both agree. Thus if the status of the architect's practice changes, there needs to be agreement with the client that the contract is novated to the new practice. Novation in this circumstance is not usually a problem, but merely a formality. Relevant circumstances include:

- partnership changes
- changes from a sole practitioner or partnership to a limited liability company, plc or limited partnership
- a change in the name of a limited liability company etc.
- a practice takeover, amalgamation or break-up.

Care needs to be taken that PII cover extends to both the original practice and the new practice.

Further reading

*The Architect's Contract. A Guide to RIBA Forms of Appointment 1999 and other Architect's Appointments, pp 44–54 (RIBA Publications, 1999).
M. Lenihan and J. Redmond To 'B' or 'D&B'? Design and Build in the 90s (Society of Construction Law, 1994).
*D. Mosey Design and Build in Action (Chandos, 1998).

Notes

1 D. Mosey Design and Build in Action, p 48 (Chandos, 1998).
2 M. Lenihan and J. Redmond To 'B' or 'D&B'? Design and Build in the 90s, p 15 (Society of Construction Law, 1994).
3 Tesco Stores Ltd v Norman Hiscox Partnership [1998] 56 Con LR 42.

Index

developer's profit
 – share of   110
development monitoring   94
disbursements   110
dispute resolution   77, 88
dispute resolution services   67
disruption   66
 – charging for   109
 – by others   109
documentation   135
 – need for consistency   95
double novation   133
drains   67
drawings
 – checking of   93
 – revisions of   65
 – special   64
dutch auction   104
duty of care   71
 – in tort   134

easement   68
Employer's Agent   43, 45, 83
Employer's Requirements   43, 44, 80
energy audits   63
environmental studies   62
equipment   105
estimates of cost   79
expenses   110
experience   78, 102
expert
 – terms of engagement   89
expert determinator   88
 – indemnity of   88
expert witness   88
extensions of time   65
extra work   109

facilities management   94
facilities manager
 – architect as   94

feasibility studies   62, 67
fee agreement
 – tailoring of   70
fee assessments   101
fee bids   27
fee competition   20
fee cutting   103
fee scales
 – indicative   107
fee tender deadlines   19
feedback   68
fees   101
 – comparisons of   107
 – estimates of   101
 – for variations   102
 – graphs of   101
 – low   104
 – lump sum   107
 – methods of establishing   69
 – multi disciplinary   102
 – percentage   104
 – reduction of   103
 – stage payments of   105
 – time basis   108
 – time of payment   101
 – undercutting   104
finance charges   101
financial resources   26
fire damage   67
fitness for purpose   54, 71
furniture & fittings
 – design of   64
 – selection of   64

gentlemen's agreement   71
grant applications   64
grant-aided works   65
grants   86
ground investigations   62
group practice   8
Guide to RIBA Forms of Appointment
 85, 108